Fuel

Your

Day!

Recipe pictured on page 182

Madame Labriski

Dairy- and Gluten-Free Options for Every Recipe!

No Added Sugar or Fat!

FUEL YOUR DAY!

100+ Seriously Addictive Energy Cookies, Bites, Bars & More

madamelabriski.com

appetite
by RANDOM HOUSE

Appetite by Random House® and colophon are registered trademarks of Penguin Random House LLC.

Library and Archives of Canada Cataloguing in Publication is available upon request.

ISBN: 978-0-525-61030-4
eBook ISBN: 978-0-525-61031-1

Cover and book photography: Jean-François Frenette and Brigitte Thériault
Translated by Marie Asselin
Printed and bound in China

Published in Canada by Appetite by Random House®,
a division of Penguin Random House Canada Limited.

www.penguinrandomhouse.ca

10 9 8 7 6 5 4 3 2 1

To my mother,
who let me experiment in the
kitchen from a very early age.

To the lights of my life:
Antoinette, Adrien, and Philippe.

Table of Contents

Hello! Bonjour! Welcome to the world of Madame Labriski (La-bri-skee)!

Here you will find energy treats full of nutrition, energy, yumminess, and fun, fun, funski!!

Introduction

Recipes free of refined sugar and fat (and gluten and dairy, if you want!)— and full of flavor and happiness!

Welcome, it's wonderful to meet you! I am Madame Labriski of madamelabriski.com, and my mission is to energize the world! I'm the creator of the most tasty and energy-fuelling treats you will ever eat—so popular that they are the talk of the town! In French Canada this cookbook was a bestseller that flew off the shelves, and I am thrilled that English readers will now discover my delicious energy treats and so much moreski.

Let me tell you a little bit more about me . . . In my real life, I am a mother, an entrepreneur, and a marathon runner (with a personal best of 3 hours and 8 minutes, but who knows after my next marathon!?) A few years ago, I was looking for 100% healthy energizing snack that would fuel me up before my workouts and also satisfy my sweet tooth. Frustrated by a fruitless search, I decided to take matters into my own hands, and have a go at making yummy treats without adding any refined sugar or fat. My first project was to develop an energy cookie based on a classic cookie—because who doesn't like cookies? My kitchen became a sort of delicious culinary laboratory as I began to experiment with different ways to make healthy treats also yummy. And finally, after a lot of trial and error . . . voilà! My energy cookie was born!

Inspired, I decided to keep going and expand to happy, healthy snacks for my whole family. I developed recipes for energy bites, bars, muffins, and even cakes. I'm proud that all my recipes are chock-full of health benefits, naturally sweetened, incredibly flavorful, and packed with fiber. Joy-inspiring treats without added sugar or fat? It can be doneski!

But how did you do it, Madame Labriski, you might ask? The secret is swapping out sugar for my "magical" date puree, combining it with either nonfat plain yogurt or unsweetened applesauce, and then adding your choice of flavors. So . . . does that mean they taste like cardboard? Not at all. They are surprisingly delicious, and even better, they're easy to make.

This book begins with an overview of the ingredients and equipment you need to make my treats (surprise, very littleski!) and then I share my recipe for homemade magical date puree. After that, we're off to the races with eight chapters of easy recipes for a variety of healthy energy-filled treats to help you fuel your and your family's busy days.

When it comes to healthy and yummy eating, it's easy to take ourselves too seriously and forget to laugh. But making energy treats is funski! So, I like to get creative with my recipe titles, because why not? You can start your morning with the Lightness of Being (see page 26), recover from your workout with a Date with Destiny (see page 95), and impress your family and friends with an I Love Me a Mishmash (see page 192)! Also, keep an eye out for the many helpful tips I've sprinkled throughout the book—my Tipskis!

So grab your wooden spoons, your mixing bowls, and your ingredients. It's time to make some (you know what I'm going to say . . .) treatskis!

Have Fun!

Madame Labriski

Madame Labriski = yummy, healthy funski!!

Making My Energy Treats Is Simple!

**Do you have a sweet tooth?
Do you want delicious, indulgent snacks
without the guilt? Then you're going
to want to make energy treats with
Madame Labriski!**

My energy treats have no added sugar or fat—instead they are sweetened with
date puree and loaded with fiber (even the most decadent ones). They are 100%
healthy and will make you want to live your life to the fullest. Who said healthy
cooking had to be complicated?

Q: Really, No Added Sugar or Fat?

Ok, fine—I cheat a little sometimes. The dough contains no
added sugar or fat, but you will occasionally spot chocolate
or caramel chips in my recipes. When I first started making
my energy treats, I wanted to avoid these kinds of ingredients at all costs. But a nutritionist friend told me that in
cooking, as in life, it all comes down to balance. So the
choice is yours: if you want to include those ingredients, go
for it, but if you don't, you can always just leave them out.

TIPSKI!

For a healthy choice,
opt for dark chocolate
chips (75% cocoa
content or higher).

Q: What about Me? I Eat Gluten-Free & Dairy-Free!

All the recipes in this book can be made without gluten or dairy products. Yes,
really!

For gluten-free treats, simply substitute the other flours with your favorite gluten-free variety available at your grocery store. For dairy-free, use store-bought unsweetened applesauce instead of nonfat plain yogurt. There is no need to hunt for complicated ingredients—simpleski!

Q: How about Calories?

Lots of people have asked for my recipes' nutritional information, including calorie count. But because I'm not a trained nutritionist or a dietitian (I'm just a woman who has big ideas to change the world, one energy treat at a time!), this isn't information I'm focused on. I've chosen not to count the calories of the food I eat. After all, they're just a number! Are the recipes in this book low-calorie? No. They are healthy, easy-to-make recipes that are packed with ingredients to provide lasting energy. Deciding to eat healthily is a choice. The great thing about making these energy treats is that you choose what you put in the recipe and, therefore, into your body.

Q: What about Recipes for Athletes?

Yes! As a marathon runner, I spent a long time looking for healthy, energy-boosting snacks to fuel up with before my running sessions—and I ended up making them myself (page 81)! I have also created post-workout cookies that allow you to cut down on your recovery time (page 101).

Q: Do You Have School Lunch–Appropriate Recipes My Kids Will Love (No Nuts, No Chocolate, and for those who have allergies, No Dairy)?

Yes! My children absolutely love my cookies, and yours will too. On page 87, you'll even find a healthy, homemade version of the popular Bear Paws cookies.

Making my energy treats is easy! Think you can't cook? Then these recipes are perfect for you! Simply put the ingredients in a bowl, mix, bake, let cool, and then enjoy. Ta-da! Honestly, that's all you need to know to make these cookies.

Warning:

These energy treats may be addictive.

You may want to eat them all day, every day, morning, noon, and night.

(Don't say I didn't warn you!)

On Your Mark, Get Set . . . Go!

When you cook with joy, you spread joy to those around you!

In the kitchen, as in life, everything comes down to attitude and energy. Over the years, I've noticed something interesting: when I'm in a good mood in the kitchen, my culinary creations turn out better. To turn your own kitchen into a delicious and healthy energy treat bakery, you'll need a few basic pieces of equipment and pantry itemski.

What You Need

Wooden spoon
2 small or large spoons (to portion the cookies and place them on the baking sheet), or an ice-cream scoop (see page 13)
Measuring cup

Measuring spoons
Baking sheet
Large mixing bowl
Muffin pan
Round 7-inch (18 cm) cake pan
12 x 5-inch (30 x 13 cm) loaf pan

What's helpful to have?
Silicone mat or parchment paper to line your baking sheet or muffin pan with (it prevents the cookies and muffins from sticking)

What's handy to have?
Cooling rack (you can find this at a dollar store)

What's optional?
Scale (weighing ingredients can save time, but it's not necessary)

What's essential?
The ingredients for the recipe, and—most importantly—your sense of fun!

TIPSKI!

Want to make perfectly
shaped cookies? Use an
ice-cream (or cookie)
scoop to shape them:
½ oz (15 g) = bite size
1 oz (30 g) = snack size
2½ oz (70 g) = king size

Pantry Basics to Have on Hand

- Dried pitted dates
- Nonfat plain yogurt or unsweetened applesauce (they're interchangeable and both available at your local grocery store)
- Baking soda
- Baking powder
- Salt

- Flour (wheat, spelt, kamut, oat, quinoa, etc., in either the regular or gluten-free variety, whichever you prefer)
- Chia seeds or flaxseeds (they're interchangeable)
- Quick-cooking rolled oats
- Dried fruits, chocolate chips, and whatever else suits your fancy!

Storing Energy Treats

All of my creations are better once they've cooled to room temperature. They're even better the next day. When it's time to pack them away, forget the cookie jar! These treats should be kept in the fridge or freezer, in an airtight container to maximize their freshness. They will keep for:

- 1 week in the fridge
- 3 months in the freezer

But . . . everyone tells me it's impossible to make them last for a whole week—because they'll be devoured long before that! Good luck!

TIPSKI!

For the best flavor, freeze overripe bananas. When you're ready to make cookies, zap frozen bananas in the microwave for 1 minute and toss them into your recipe.

Be creative and trust yourself!

TIPSKI!

Want to be dairy-free? Simply, substitute the yogurt listed in the recipes for unsweetened applesauce. Isn't that amazing?

Dates: The Love of My Life

Ah, dates—those little packages of goodness for your body.

Why should you sweeten foods with date puree? Because dates are delicious! They are also rich in fiber and are an excellent source of natural sugar. Trust me, you'll really love them.

Did I try using any other dried fruits? Yes, yes, and yes! I tried everything, believe me! I tested raisins, dried apricots, prunes, and figs—but the all-around winners (in terms of value for money, yield, and flavor) are dates. What if you don't like dates? Well, I have good news for you: dates have the most neutral taste, so they can complement any flavor you add to your energy treatski. (Quick! Look to the opposite page to find out how to make your own date puree at home.)

Dates sure are delicious, but they also have lots of health benefits. They are:

- An excellent source of energy for physical activity!
- Rich in fiber, to help ward off constipation and optimize digestion!
- High in vitamin A, to help regenerate corneas and protect eyes!
- Rich in potassium, to help prevent cardiovascular disease and reduce cholesterol!

They also:

- Boost liver function when consumed on a regular basis!
- Clean out your arteries, to improve long-term health!

So what are you waiting for? Look to the page opposite and make a date with dates!

Date Puree

How do you make date puree? Simpleski! This one recipe has three very straightforward methods for you to choose from. Just pick what works best for you—and have fun!

2½ cups (750 g) date puree, or 5 servings of ½ cup (150 g) each
PREPARATION TIME: about 25 minutes
COOKING TIME: 4 minutes in the microwave, 8 minutes on the stovetop

3 cups (500 g) dried pitted dates
1⅔ cups (410 ml) water
That's it!

IN THE MICROWAVE Put the dates and water in a microwave-safe container and cook for 4 minutes.

ON THE STOVETOP In a saucepan, bring the dates and water to a boil and simmer on medium heat until they're very soft, about 8 minutes.

COUNTERTOP If you have the time, put the dates in the water in a bowl and let them soak on the countertop for 24 hours.

And then what?

Mix everything with a hand blender (zoom, zoom!) or stir vigorously with a wooden spoon until you get a smooth, pureed consistency. You're looking for a texture like Greek yogurt. If you can stand a spoon in the mixture, it's perfect. Great job! You've now got a delicious date puree!

STORAGE Keeps for 2 weeks in an airtight container in the fridge, or in the freezer for up to 3 months.

TIPSKI!

To save time, divide the puree into ½ cup (150 g) portions before freezing. Don't worry if they don't completely harden in the freezer, this is completely normal.

Are you making treats yet?

Great!

I bet your home smells wonderfulski!

Cock-a-Doodle-Go Go Goooooo!

Life's a marathon. From morning to night, we never stop. Work, work, work, exercise, kids, meals, homework—ouchski! Do you have time to stop and have a healthy breakfast every day? I bet you don't, but that's no excuse to inhale empty calorie–filled pastries on the run. Such treats don't provide the energy you need to sustain your crazy schedule. For those of you in a hurry, I created recipes that will allow you to start your morning right. Enjoy your crazy day!

1

Recipes for Busy Mornings

The Good Morning Banana

(banana, pecan, and wheat bran cookies)

Gooooood morning! This cookie is a source of fiber and will make your busy mornings happy and sunny. Big appetite this morning? Spread on a little natural peanut or almond butter for a more filling treat.

MAKES 17 energy cookies, 1 oz (30 g) each
OVEN TEMPERATURE: 350°F (180°C)   **COOKING TIME:** 15 minutes

¾ cup (225 g) date puree
½ cup (150 g) nonfat plain yogurt or unsweetened applesauce
1 very ripe banana, mashed
1 egg

1 tablespoon (15 ml) pure vanilla extract
½ teaspoon (2 ml) baking soda
1 teaspoon (5 ml) baking powder
Pinch of salt

1 cup (150 g) whole grain spelt flour
½ cup (50 g) wheat bran
⅓ cup (40 g) quick-cooking rolled oats
⅓ cup (40 g) ground flaxseeds
⅔ cup (80 g) pecans, coarsely chopped

Pecans, for garnish

And then what?

1   Preheat the oven to 350°F (180°C).
2   In a bowl, combine the ingredients from the **orange** section.
3   Add the ingredients from the **blue** section. Wait for a light frothing to occur (just for fun), then mix well.
4   Gradually mix in the ingredients from the **pink** section until combined.
5   Line a baking sheet with parchment paper or a silicone mat—otherwise, everything will stick.
6   Drop spoonfuls of dough to create beautifully round energy cookies.
7   Decorate each cookie with a whole or half pecan. This will make them cuter and even more delicious!
8   Bake for about 15 minutes. Transfer the baked cookies to a cooling rack, and bask in their mouthwatering aroma.

The Granolita
(raisin, coconut, and oat cookies)
page 26

The Hello Blue . . . tiful
(oat, wheat bran, and blueberry muffins)
page 27

The Lightness of Being
(wheat bran and date muffins)
page 26

The Van Go
(raisin and sunflower seed cookies)
page 28

The Orange-inal
(orange juice and date cookies)
page 28

The Mahhhtcha
(matcha oat cookies)
page 29

The Granolita

(raisin, coconut, and oat cookies)

I smile every time I say the name of these nourishing cookies. Granolita! Granolita! Doesn't it sound like the name of an Italian *nonna* who'd bake these cookies? I bet she'd fill them with love. Enjoy your delicious day!

MAKES 20 energy cookies, 1 oz (30 g) each
OVEN TEMPERATURE: 350°F (180°C)
COOKING TIME: 12 minutes

½ cup (150 g) date puree
½ cup (150 g) nonfat plain yogurt
⅓ cup (80 ml) water
1 egg

2 tablespoons (30 ml) pure vanilla extract
½ teaspoon (2 ml) baking soda
1 teaspoon (5 ml) baking powder
Pinch of salt

1 cup (150 g) whole wheat flour
1½ cups (150 g) large flake oats
½ cup (50 g) wheat bran
¼ cup (25 g) toasted wheat germ
¼ cup (30 g) ground flaxseeds
¾ cup (100 g) Thompson raisins
¾ cup (75 g) unsweetened shredded
   coconut
½ cup (60 g) chopped walnuts

The Lightness of Being

(wheat bran and date muffins)

Feeling feather-light after gobbling down a big breakfast is wonderful! Perfect with your favorite hot beverage, this muffin is jam-packed with fiber. Make these whenever you feel the need.

MAKES 12 muffins
OVEN TEMPERATURE: 350°F (180°C)
COOKING TIME: 17 minutes

½ cup (150 g) date puree
½ cup (150 g) unsweetened applesauce
1 egg

1 teaspoon (5 ml) pure vanilla extract
½ teaspoon (2 ml) baking soda
1 tablespoon (15 ml) baking powder
Pinch of salt

1 cup (150 g) whole wheat flour
1 cup (100 g) wheat bran
1 cup (160 g) dried pitted dates, or 1 cup
   (200 g) dried pitted prunes
¼ cup (30 g) ground flaxseeds

All recipes pictured on page 24

The Hello Blue . . . tiful

(wheat bran and blueberry muffins)

Ahoy-hoy! Bonjour, bonjour! Hola, hola! Hello, hello, blue . . . tiful! If you love blueberry muffins, you'll go wild for this healthy, energy-packed morning solution that will make you put away your favorite cereals forever.

MAKES 8 muffins
OVEN TEMPERATURE: 350°F (180°C)
COOKING TIME: 18 minutes

½ cup (150 g) date puree
½ cup (150 g) nonfat plain yogurt
1 egg

1 tablespoon (15 ml) pure vanilla extract
½ teaspoon (2 ml) baking soda
1½ teaspoons (7 ml) baking powder
Pinch of salt

½ cup (75 g) whole grain spelt flour or
    another type of flour
½ cup (50 g) wheat bran
¼ cup (30 g) ground flaxseeds
1 cup (150 g) fresh or frozen blueberries

And then what? ● ● ● ● ● ● ● ● ● ● ● ● ▶

1 Preheat the oven to 350°F (180°C).
2 In a bowl, combine the ingredients from the **orange** section.
3 Add the ingredients from the blue section. Wait for a light frothing to occur (just for fun), then mix well.
4 Mix in the ingredients from the **pink** section until fully combined.
5 For the Granolita, line a baking sheet with parchment or a silicone mat. For the others, line a muffin pan with parchment paper or silicone liners. If you don't have liners, grease the pan —otherwise, everything will stick.
6 For the Granolita, drop spoonfuls of dough onto the pan, to create beautifully round energy cookies. For the others, divide the mixture evenly among the muffin cups.
7 Decorate as desired!
8 Bake for the time indicated. Transfer to a cooling rack, and bask in their mouthwatering aroma. Enjoy!

The Orange-inal

(orange juice and date cookies)

What's this? An orange juice cookie made with orange juice concentrate that's also 100% delicious? Yes, please! This energy cookie is extremely simple to make, and its fresh taste is so good in the mornings!

MAKES 20 energy cookies, 1 oz (30 g) each
OVEN TEMPERATURE: 350°F (180°C)
COOKING TIME: 15 minutes

½ cup (150 g) date puree
½ cup (150 g) frozen orange juice
    concentrate
1 egg

½ teaspoon (2 ml) baking soda
1½ teaspoons (7 ml) baking powder
Pinch of salt

1 cup (150 g) regular or gluten-free
    all-purpose flour
¼ cup (25 g) almond flour
¼ cup (40 g) chia seeds
½ cup (80 g) dried pitted dates, chopped

The Van Go

(raisin and sunflower seed cookies)

Imagine a field of sunflowers bathed in sunlight. Gorgeous, isn't it? This is the Van Go: an energy cookie that celebrates sunflower seeds, which are a great source of fiber and energy that's also packed with sunshine!

MAKES 12 energy cookies, 1 oz (30 g each)
OVEN TEMPERATURE: 350°F (180°C)
COOKING TIME: 15 minutes

½ cup (150 g) date puree
½ cup (150 g) unsweetened applesauce
1 egg

1 tablespoon (15 ml) pure vanilla extract
½ teaspoon (2 ml) baking soda
½ teaspoon (2 ml) baking powder
Pinch of salt

¾ cup (115 g) oat flour
¾ cup (75 g) quick-cooking rolled oats
¼ cup (25 g) wheat bran
¼ cup (40 g) chia seeds
¼ cup (30 g) ground flaxseeds
½ cup (60 g) shelled sunflower seeds
½ cup (65 g) raisins

All recipes pictured on page 25

The Mahhhtcha

(matcha oat cookies)

Matcha, mahhhtcha! The taste of this green tea powder, which is packed with a ton of nutrients and antioxidants, makes me giddy. With Mahhhtcha, your mornings will be full of vitality. Take Madame Labriski's word for it!

MAKES 12 energy cookies, 1 oz (30 g) each
OVEN TEMPERATURE: 350°F (180°C)
COOKING TIME: 15 minutes

½ cup (150 g) date puree
½ cup (150 g) unsweetened applesauce
¼ cup (60 ml) cow's, almond, or soy milk
1 egg

1 tablespoon (15 ml) pure vanilla extract
½ teaspoon (2 ml) baking soda
1 tablespoon (15 ml) baking powder
1 to 3 tablespoons (15 to 45 ml) powdered
    matcha tea

1 cup (150 g) oat flour
¾ cup (75 g) quick-cooking rolled oats
2 tablespoons (30 ml) chia seeds
½ cup (100 g) white chocolate chips
    (optional)

And then what? ● ● ● ● ● ● ● ● ● ● ➤

1   Preheat the oven to 350°F (180°C).
2   In a bowl, combine the ingredients from the **orange** section.
3   Add the ingredients from the blue section. Wait for a light frothing to occur (just for fun), then mix well.
4   Mix in the ingredients from the **pink** section until fully combined.
5   Line a baking sheet with parchment paper or a silicone mat—otherwise, everything will stick.
6   Drop spoonfuls of dough to create beautifully round energy cookies, and decorate as desired.
7   Bake for about 15 minutes. Your kitchen will soon smell like happiness! Your challenge? Waiting until the cookies are cool before eating them. They're just so good!

The Mediterranean Blue

(blueberry and lemon zest muffins)

A quiet morning + a terrace on the Mediterranean + a Mediterranean Blue muffin = a vacation! The Mediterranean Blue is a fluffy treat full of blueberries, and I just love its delicate lemony aroma. This muffin is made to travel and will sweep you off your feet.

MAKES 12 muffins   **OVEN TEMPERATURE:** 350°F (180°C)   **COOKING TIME:** 40 minutes

½ cup (150 g) date puree
¾ cup (185 ml) cow's, almond, or soy
   milk
1 egg

1 tablespoon (15 ml) pure vanilla extract
½ teaspoon (2 ml) baking soda
2 teaspoons (10 ml) baking powder
Finely grated zest of 1 lemon
Pinch of salt

1 cup (150 g) flour of your choice
   (excellent with gluten-free flour!)
¼ cup (40 g) chia seeds
1 cup (150 g) fresh or frozen blueberries

And then what?

1   Preheat the oven to 350°F (180°C).
2   In a bowl, combine the ingredients from the orange section.
3   Add the ingredients from the blue section. Wait for a light frothing to occur (just for fun), then mix well.
4   Mix in the ingredients from the **pink** section until fully combined.
5   Line a muffin pan with parchment paper or silicone liners. If you don't have liners, lightly grease the pan—otherwise, everything will stick.
6   Divide the mixture evenly among the muffin cups.
7   Bake for about 40 minutes. Yum! Smells like happiness!

The Un-Beet-Able

(raw beet powder, quinoa, and pumpkin seed cookies)

This energy cookie is gluten-free and rich in nitrates, thanks to the raw beet powder, making it a perfect morning solution for athletes. It seems that nitrates can improve endurance and physical performance. As for quinoa flour, I just looooove it! Have one every morning!

MAKES 24 cookies, 1 oz (30 g) each **OVEN TEMPERATURE:** 350°F (180°C) **COOKING TIME:** 15 minutes

½ cup (150 g) date puree
½ cup (150 g) unsweetened applesauce
2 eggs

1½ teaspoons (7 ml) pure vanilla
  extract
½ teaspoon (2 ml) baking soda
1 tablespoon (15 ml) baking powder

½ cup (65 g) quinoa flour
⅓ cup (50 g) raw beet powder
  (dehydrated beets)
¼ cup (40 g) chia seeds
½ cup (65 g) shelled green pumpkin
  seeds
½ cup (100 g) white chocolate chips

And then what?

1 Preheat the oven to 350°F (180°C).
2 In a bowl, combine the ingredients from the **orange** section.
3 Add the ingredients from the **blue** section. Wait for a light frothing to occur (just for fun), then mix well.
4 Mix in the ingredients from the **pink** section until fully combined.
5 Line a baking sheet with parchment paper or a silicone mat—otherwise, everything will stick.
6 Drop spoonfuls of dough to create beautifully round energy cookies and decorate as desired.
7 Bake for about 15 minutes. Transfer the baked cookies to a cooling rack, and bask in their mouthwatering aroma. These purple cookies are filled with goodness.

TIPSKI!:
RAW BEET POWDER

This super purple miracle
ingredient can be found in
health food stores or in
the organic section of
your favorite grocery
store.

The Bran New Day

(raisin and wheat bran muffins)

These bran-tastic muffins are way better than anything store-bought—seriously. They're also a nice way to add a little pepski to your busy mornings.

MAKES 12 muffins   **OVEN TEMPERATURE:** 350°F (180°C)   **COOKING TIME:** 30 minutes

½ cup (150 g) date puree
½ cup (150 g) unsweetened applesauce
1 cup (250 ml) cow's, almond, or soy milk
¼ cup (60 ml) blackstrap or fancy molasses
2 eggs

½ teaspoon (2 ml) baking soda
1½ teaspoons (7 ml) baking powder
Pinch of salt

1 cup (150 g) regular or gluten-free all-purpose flour
1½ cups (150 g) wheat bran
½ cup (65 g) raisins

And then what?

1   Preheat the oven to 350°F (180°C).
2   In a bowl, combine the ingredients from the **orange** section.
3   Add the ingredients from the blue section. Wait for a light frothing to occur (just for fun), then mix well.
4   Mix in the ingredients from the **pink** section until fully combined.
5   Line a muffin pan with parchment paper or silicone liners. If you don't have liners, lightly grease the pan—otherwise, everything will stick.
6   Divide the mixture evenly among the muffin cups and decorate as desired.
7   Bake for about 30 minutes. Transfer the baked muffins to a cooling rack, and bask in their mouthwatering aroma.

Getting creative in the kitchen is so much funski!

Grab your wooden spoons!

These Recipes Are Making Me S-peach-less!

Yes, these recipes are literally peachless! There's *muffin* like a good pun. Get it?!

In all seriousness, these are my classic fruit- and fiber-filled recipes. They're just so delicious that I had to put them into one chapter—oh, and you may even stumble upon a pun or two! So, how about a quick The I'm So (Straw)berry Into You (see page 47) for the roadski?

2

Recipes Packed with Fruit and Fiber

The Bomba Rosa

(raspberry, dark chocolate, and coconut cookies)

This is one of my star recipes. It just makes me want to yell out "BOMBA! BOMBA!" Why? Because it's a bomb of fruity flavors that will delight your taste buds. Go out and pick your own berries, and make this recipe as a family. It's a hit—Madame Labriski guaranteed!

MAKES 20 energy cookies, 1 oz (30 g) each
OVEN TEMPERATURE: 350°F (180°C) **COOKING TIME:** 20 minutes

½ cup (150 g) date puree
½ cup (150 g) nonfat plain yogurt
1 egg

1 tablespoon (15 ml) pure vanilla extract
½ teaspoon (2 ml) baking soda
1 ½ teaspoons (7 ml) baking powder
Pinch of salt

1 cup (100 g) quick-cooking rolled oats
1 cup (150 g) oat flour or another type
    of flour
2 tablespoons (30 ml) ground flaxseeds
½ cup (50 g) unsweetened shredded
    coconut
½ to 1 cup (100 to 200 g) dark
    chocolate chips
1 cup (150 g) fresh raspberries

And then what?

1   Preheat the oven to 350°F (180°C).
2   In a bowl, combine the ingredients from the **orange** section.
3   Add the ingredients from the **blue** section. Wait for a light frothing to occur (just for fun), then mix well.
4   Gradually mix in the ingredients from the **pink** section until fully combined.
5   Line a baking sheet with parchment paper or a silicone mat—otherwise, everything will stick.
6   Drop spoonfuls of dough to create beautifully round energy cookies and decorate as desired.
7   Bake for about 20 minutes. Get ready: your kitchen will soon smell deliciously good!

The Spotted Lemon

(lemon and poppy seed cookies)

These fresh energy cookies will make snack time feel like spring-time . . . all year round. Here's some friendly advice: to maximize this recipe's wow-factor and delicious zestiness, use pastry flour.

MAKES 20 energy cookies, 1 oz (30 g) each
OVEN TEMPERATURE: 350°F (180°C)   **COOKING TIME:** 15 minutes

½ cup (150 g) date puree
½ cup (150 g) unsweetened applesauce
2 tablespoons (30 ml) lemon juice
1 egg

1 tablespoon (15 ml) pure vanilla extract
½ teaspoon (2 ml) baking soda
1½ teaspoons (7 ml) baking powder
Finely grated zest of 2 lemons
Pinch of salt

1 cup (150 g) white pastry flour
½ cup (50 g) almond flour
1 tablespoon (15 ml) chia or poppy
  seeds

And then what?

1   Preheat the oven to 350°F (180°C).

2   In a bowl, combine the ingredients from the **orange** section.

3   Add the ingredients from the **blue** section. Wait for a light frothing to occur (after adding the lemon juice), then mix well.

4   Mix in the ingredients from the **pink** section until combined.

5   Line a baking sheet with parchment paper or a silicone mat—otherwise, everything will stick.

6   Drop spoonfuls of dough to create beautifully round energy cookies. Decorate as desired, lemon pieces look pretty!

7   Bake for about 15 minutes. Transfer the baked cookies to a cooling rack, and bask in their mouthwatering aroma.

The Oo-Lâlâ

(peanut butter and blueberry cookies)

This is one of the most popular recipes on my blog! As flavorful as it is chewy, this cookie is even better if you pronounce it with the central Quebec, Saguenay French accent. "Oo lâlâ" becomes "Oo law-law"! So, is that where I'm from? Not even close—I just like the sound of it!

MAKES 15 energy cookies, 1 oz (30 g) each
OVEN TEMPERATURE: 350°F (180°C)   **COOKING TIME:** 17 minutes

½ cup (150 g) date puree
½ cup (150 g) nonfat plain yogurt
½ cup (150 g) natural peanut butter
1 egg

1 tablespoon (15 ml) pure vanilla extract
½ teaspoon (2 ml) baking soda
1½ teaspoons (7 ml) baking powder
Pinch of salt

1 cup (150 g) spelt flour
¼ cup (30 g) ground flaxseeds
1 cup (150 g) fresh blueberries

And then what?

1   Preheat the oven to 350°F (180°C).

2   In a bowl, combine the ingredients from the **orange** section.

3   Add the ingredients from the **blue** section. Wait for a light frothing to occur (just for fun), then mix well.

4   Mix in the ingredients from the **pink** section until combined.

5   Line a baking sheet with parchment paper or a silicone mat—otherwise, everything will stick.

6   Drop spoonfuls of dough to create beautifully round energy cookies.

7   Bake for about 17 minutes. Transfer the baked cookies to a cooling rack, and bask in their mouthwatering aroma. Such a delightful treat. *Délicieux!* Delicious!

The I'm So (Straw)berry Into You

(strawberry and almond cookies)

Warning: this recipe will make your whole house smell like strawberry pie. This energy cookie is a perfect summertime treat. You will be so (straw)berry into it. Really? Oh, yes, really!

MAKES 16 energy cookies, 1 oz (30 g) each
OVEN TEMPERATURE: 350°F (180°C)   **COOKING TIME:** 22 minutes

½ cup (150 g) date puree
⅓ cup (100 g) nonfat plain yogurt
1 egg

1 tablespoon (15 ml) pure almond extract
½ teaspoon (2 ml) baking soda
1½ teaspoons (7 ml) baking powder
Pinch of salt

⅓ cup (35 g) almond flour
⅔ cup (65 g) slivered almonds
1 cup (150 g) kamut flour or another type of flour
1 cup (150 g) chopped fresh strawberries

And then what?

1   Preheat the oven to 350°F (180°C).
2   In a bowl, combine the ingredients from the **orange** section.
3   Add the ingredients from the blue section. Wait for a light frothing to occur (just for fun), then mix well.
4   Gradually mix in the ingredients from the **pink** section until combined.
5   Line a baking sheet with parchment paper or a silicone mat—otherwise, everything will stick.
6   Drop spoonfuls of dough to create beautifully round energy cookies. Decorate as desired, like a fresh strawberry slice on top.
7   Bake for about 22 minutes. Transfer the baked cookies to a cooling rack, and bask in their mouthwatering aroma. So good it tastes like *Looooooove!*

The Appley Ever After

(apple and cinnamon cookies)

These mega-healthy, soft, and chewy energy cookies will remind you of apple turnovers. Someone had to invent them! You can eat them guilt-free any time of the day. Mmmski!

MAKES 25 energy cookies, 1 oz (30 g) each
OVEN TEMPERATURE: 350°F (180°C)   **COOKING TIME:** 20 minutes

4 apples, peeled and chopped, plus
    extra for garnish
1 teaspoon (5 ml) olive oil
¼ teaspoon (1 ml) ground nutmeg
½ teaspoon (2 ml) ground cinnamon

½ cup (150 g) date puree
½ cup (150 g) unsweetened applesauce
1 egg

2 tablespoons (30 ml) apple juice
½ teaspoon (2 ml) baking soda
2 tablespoons (30 ml) baking powder
1 tablespoon (15 ml) ground cinnamon
Pinch of salt

1 cup (150 g) spelt flour or another
    type of flour
½ cup (75 g) oat flour
¼ cup (30 g) ground flaxseeds
½ cup (65 g) raisins (optional)

And then what?

1   Preheat the oven to broil.
2   Combine all the ingredients from the **orange** section in a mixing bowl.
3   Line a baking sheet with parchment paper or a silicone mat. Spread the apple mixture over the pan. Bake for 5 minutes, then set aside to cool.
4   Lower the oven temperature to 350°F (180°C).
5   Combine the ingredients from the **blue** section in a bowl.
6   Add the ingredients from the **pink** section. Wait for a light frothing to occur (just for fun), then mix well.
7   Mix in the ingredients from the **green** section and the cooled apple mixture from the **orange** section until combined.
8   Line a baking sheet with parchment paper or a silicone mat—otherwise, everything will stick.
9   Drop spoonfuls of dough to create beautifully round energy cookies.
10 Bake for about 20 minutes. Yummy!

The Alohaaaa Pina Coladaaaa

(pineapple, rum, and coconut cookies)

These cookies are simply scrumptious. With such a silly name, you can't help but love baking them. They're a source of tropical delight, and each bite feels like a stroll along the beach. *Alohaaaa!*

MAKES 20 energy cookies, 1 oz (30 g) each
OVEN TEMPERATURE: 350°F (180°C)   **COOKING TIME:** 15 minutes

One 14 oz (398 ml) can pineapple
½ cup (150 g) date puree
1 egg

1 tablespoon (15 ml) spiced rum or
   artificial rum extract
1 teaspoon (5 ml) baking soda
1 tablespoon (15 ml) baking powder
Pinch of salt

1 cup (150 g) gluten-free flour or
   another type of flour
¼ cup (40 g) chia seeds
½ cup (50 g) unsweetened shredded
   coconut
½ cup (40 g) store-bought toasted
   coconut slices

And then what?

1   Preheat the oven to 350°F (180°C).
2   Puree the pineapple to a smooth consistency using a hand blender (zoom, zoom!).
3   In a bowl, combine the ingredients from the **orange** section.
4   Add the ingredients from the **blue** section. Wait for a light frothing to occur (just for fun), then mix well.
5   Mix in the ingredients from the **pink** section until combined.
6   Line a baking sheet with parchment paper or a silicone mat—otherwise, everything will stick.
7   Drop spoonfuls of dough to create beautifully round energy cookies. Decorate as desired.
8   Bake for about 15 minutes. Transfer the baked cookies to a cooling rack, and bask in their mouthwatering aroma. What a fiesta! *C'est la fête!*

The Berry Nice Things

(raspberry and Crystal Light cookies)

This unique cookie is surprisingly juicy. Its secret is that it's made with a packet of Raspberry Ice Crystal Light brand drink mix. Now, surely I wouldn't dare! Well, yes, I did . . . and the result is deliciouski.

MAKES 20 energy cookies, 1 oz (30 g) each
OVEN TEMPERATURE: 350°F (180°C)   **COOKING TIME:** 18 minutes

½ cup (150 g) date puree
½ cup (150 g) unsweetened applesauce
or pureed berries
1 egg

One 0.8 oz (2.4 g) packet of Raspberry
Ice Crystal Light
½ teaspoon (2 ml) baking soda
1½ teaspoons (7 ml) baking powder
Pinch of salt

1¼ cups (185 g) gluten-free flour or
another type of flour
¼ cup (30 g) ground flaxseeds
½ cup (125 g) frozen raspberries

And then what?

1   Preheat the oven to 350°F (180°C).

2   In a bowl, combine the ingredients from the **orange** section.

3   Add the ingredients from the **blue** section. Wait for a light frothing to occur (just for fun), then mix well.

4   Mix in the ingredients from the **pink** section until combined.

5   Line a baking sheet with parchment paper or a silicone mat—otherwise, everything will stick.

6   Drop spoonfuls of dough to create beautifully round energy cookies. Decorate as desired, fresh raspberries make them extra juicy.

7   Bake for about 18 minutes. Transfer the baked cookies to a cooling rack, and bask in their mouthwatering aroma. Enjoy life through pink-colored glasses!

The Sweet Clementine

(clementine and oat cookies)

Oh, divine clementine, with your cute little leaf, you're the fruit I most enjoy peeling. Your scent is delicious, and this energy cookie makes a perfect snack.

MAKES 16 energy cookies, 1 oz (30 g) each
OVEN TEMPERATURE: 350°F (180°C)
COOKING TIME: 15 minutes

½ cup (150 g) date puree
½ cup (150 g) unsweetened applesauce
1 egg

½ teaspoon (2 ml) baking soda
1 teaspoon (5 ml) baking powder
Finely grated zest of 3 clementines
Pinch of salt

1 cup (100 g) quick-cooking rolled oats
½ cup (75 g) oat, wheat, or spelt flour
2 tablespoons (30 ml) ground flaxseeds
½ cup (75 g) dried pitted dates, chopped

The Zest of Key West

(lime, almond, and oat cookies)

Inspired by the famous key lime pie, this creation makes you want to take a road trip from Miami to Key West. This healthy treat is irresistibly summery.

MAKES 20 energy cookies, 1 oz (30 g) each
OVEN TEMPERATURE: 350°F (180°C)
COOKING TIME: 20 minutes

½ cup (150 g) date puree
½ cup (150 g) unsweetened applesauce
1 egg

½ teaspoon (2 ml) baking soda
1 tablespoon (15 ml) baking powder
Finely grated zest of 2 large limes
1½ tablespoons (22 ml) lime juice

Pinch of salt
1 cup (100 g) almond flour
1 cup (100 g) quick-cooking rolled oats
½ cup (80 g) chia seeds
½ cup (100 g) white chocolate chips
   (optional)

The Cumulus Citrus

(blueberry and lemon zest cookies)

Gluten- and dairy-free, this cookie tastes just like a cloud. Have I ever tasted a cloud? No . . . but I can dream, can't I? These energy cookies are a source of fiber with a hint of fruit.

MAKES 15 energy cookies, 1 oz (30 g) each
OVEN TEMPERATURE: 350°F (180°C)
COOKING TIME: 15 minutes

½ cup (150 g) date puree
½ cup (150 g) unsweetened applesauce
1 egg

½ teaspoon (2 ml) baking soda
1½ teaspoons (7 ml) baking powder
1 tablespoon (15 ml) pure vanilla extract
Finely grated zest of 1 lemon
Pinch of salt

¾ cup (115 g) gluten-free flour
¼ cup (30 g) coconut flour
2 tablespoons (30 ml) ground flaxseeds
1 cup (150 g) frozen blueberries

And then what? ● · · · · · · · · · · ▶

1   Preheat the oven to 350°F (180°C).
2   In a bowl, combine the ingredients from the **orange** section.
3   Add the ingredients from the blue section. Wait for a light frothing to occur (just for fun), then mix well.
4   Mix in the ingredients from the **pink** section until combined.
5   Line a baking sheet with parchment paper or a silicone mat—otherwise, everything will stick.
6   Drop spoonfuls of dough to create beautifully round energy cookies.
7   Bake for the time indicated (either 15 or 20 minutes). Transfer the baked cookies to a cooling rack, and bask in their mouthwatering aroma.

The Oh So Strawberrylicious

(strawberry and oat cookies)

So pretty, and so good! This nut-free, dairy-free cookie makes the most of fresh strawberry season. You just want to make this recipe again and again . . . and againski.

MAKES 28 energy cookies, 1 oz (30 g) each
OVEN TEMPERATURE: 350°F (180°C)   **COOKING TIME:** 15 minutes

½ cup (150 g) date puree
½ cup (150 g) unsweetened applesauce
¼ cup (60 ml) cold water
1 egg

1 tablespoon (15 ml) pure vanilla extract
½ teaspoon (2 ml) baking soda
1½ teaspoons (7 ml) baking powder
Pinch of salt

1 cup (150 g) oat flour
¾ cup (75 g) quick-cooking rolled oats
2 tablespoons (30 ml) ground flaxseeds
16 strawberries, sliced (about
    1 cup/150 g)
½ cup (100 g) chocolate chips (optional)

And then what?

1   Preheat the oven to 350°F (180°C).

2   In a bowl, combine the ingredients from the **orange** section.

3   Add the ingredients from the blue section. Wait for a light frothing to occur (just for fun), then mix well.

4   Gradually mix in the ingredients from the **pink** section until combined.

5   Line a baking sheet with parchment paper or a silicone mat—otherwise, everything will stick.

6   Drop spoonfuls of dough to create beautifully round energy cookies. Decorate each cookie with a slice of fresh strawberry.

7   Bake for about 15 minutes. Transfer the baked cookies to a cooling rack, and bask in their mouthwatering aroma. Smells like happiness!

The Crazy Clementine

(clementine, almond, and corn flour muffins)

Having guests over for brunch? This gluten-free, dairy-free creation is sure to be a big success. It's a source of fiber, vitamins, and energy, and of course, loooooove!

MAKES 12 muffins   **OVEN TEMPERATURE:** 350°F (180°C)   **COOKING TIME:** 40 minutes

½ cup (150 g) date puree
½ cup (150 g) unsweetened applesauce
1 cup (250 ml) cow's, almond, or soy milk
1 egg

1 tablespoon (15 ml) pure almond extract
½ teaspoon (2 ml) baking soda
1 tablespoon (15 ml) baking powder
Finely grated zest of 3 clementines
Pinch of salt

1 cup (150 g) corn flour
¼ cup (30 g) raw hemp seeds, or ¼ cup (40 g) chia seeds
½ cup (50 g) slivered almonds
3 clementines, peeled and chopped

And then what?

1   Preheat the oven to 350°F (180°C).
2   In a bowl, combine the ingredients from the **orange** section.
3   Add the ingredients from the **blue** section. Wait for a light frothing to occur (just for fun), then mix well.
4   Mix in the ingredients from the **pink** section until combined.
5   Line a muffin pan with parchment paper or silicone liners. If you don't have liners, lightly grease the pan—otherwise, everything will stick.
6   Divide the mixture evenly among the muffin cups and decorate as desired.
7   Bake for about 40 minutes. Transfer the baked muffins to a cooling rack, and take in that zesty scent!

Recipes to Keep You Going, and Going, and Going . . .

These energy cookies are so tasty and good. Really good. And they'll keep you going for a long time. A really long time. They are the ultimate snack attack. You can take them on a hike or to work, or even give them as gifts (what a great idea!). These treats are not only delicious and beneficial to your health but they will also fulfill your food cravings—the healthy way! But watch out: you might make your friends jealous with these snacks . . . or better yet, even make some new ones!

3

Recipes for When You're On the Go

The Granola Deluxe
(quinoa flour and almond butter cookies)
page 64

The Iron Strength
(peanut butter and molasses cookies)
page 64

The Nice to Seed You
(multigrain cookies)
page 65

The My Darling Chickpea
(chickpea flour and
peanut butter cookies)
page 66

The You Pecan't Stop
(graham cracker crumb,
oat, and pecan cookies)
page 67

The OMG It's So Good
(peanut, almond, and chocolate cookies)
page 66

The Iron Strength

(peanut butter and molasses cookies)

Boom! This cookie is incredibly good, but it's even tastier the day after being made. It's about time someone thought of combining molasses and peanut butter!

MAKES 35 energy cookies, 1 oz (30 g) each
OVEN TEMPERATURE: 350°F (180°C)
COOKING TIME: 15 minutes

½ cup (150 g) date puree
½ cup (150 g) unsweetened applesauce
½ cup (150 g) natural peanut butter
½ cup (125 ml) blackstrap or fancy molasses
1 egg

1 teaspoon (5 ml) pure vanilla extract
¼ teaspoon (1 ml) baking soda
2 teaspoons (10 ml) baking powder

1 cup (150 g) whole wheat flour
1 cup (100 g) quick-cooking rolled oats
½ cup (75 g) unsalted peanuts, chopped or ground
¼ cup (30 g) ground flaxseeds

TIPSKI!

To triple the iron content, use organic blackstrap molasses.

The Granola Deluxe

(quinoa flour and almond butter cookies)

I just love quinoa flour. It's rich in protein and is also an excellent source of iron, zinc, magnesium, potassium, and other minerals. Full of almond butter, this cookie is a luxurious treat that's also gluten-free.

MAKES 22 energy cookies, 1 oz (30 g) each
OVEN TEMPERATURE: 350°F (180°C)
COOKING TIME: 15 minutes

½ cup (150 g) date puree
½ cup (150 g) unsweetened applesauce
½ cup (150 g) natural almond butter
1 egg

½ teaspoon (2 ml) baking soda
2 teaspoons (10 ml) baking powder
Pinch of salt

1 cup (130 g) quinoa flour
¼ cup (25 g) slivered almonds
¼ cup (50 g) chocolate chips

All recipes pictured on page 62

The Nice to Seed You

(multigrain cookies)

I bet you'll start attracting birdies to your kitchen with this deep-seeded recipe. When you're famished, there's nothing like munching on these energy cookies. Enjoy!

MAKES 16 energy cookies, 1 oz (30 g) each
OVEN TEMPERATURE: 350°F (180°C)
COOKING TIME: 15 minutes

½ cup (150 g) date puree
½ cup (150 g) nonfat plain yogurt
1 egg

¼ teaspoon (1 ml) baking soda
1 teaspoon (5 ml) baking powder
Pinch of salt

⅓ cup (35 g) wheat bran
¼ cup (25 g) toasted wheat germ
¼ cup (30 g) ground flaxseeds
¼ cup (40 g) whole wheat flour
½ cup (60 g) sesame seeds
¼ cup (40 g) chia seeds
¼ cup (30 g) shelled sunflower seeds
½ cup (65 g) dried currants

And then what? ●· · · · · · · · · · ▶

1   Preheat the oven to 350°F (180°C).
2   In a bowl, combine the ingredients from the **orange** section.
3   Add the ingredients from the **blue** section. Wait for a light frothing to occur (just for fun), then mix well.
4   Gradually mix in the ingredients from the **pink** section until combined.
5   Line a baking sheet with parchment paper or a silicone mat—otherwise, everything will stick.
6   Drop spoonfuls of dough to create beautifully round energy cookies, and decorate as desired.
7   Bake for about 15 minutes. Let cool before indulging. I'll bet you can't eat just one . . . or two . . . or just one more!

The My Darling Chickpea

(chickpea flour and peanut butter cookies)

Chickpeas have the power to transform a typical peanut butter cookie into a healthier treat thanks to their high fiber—among their many other nutritional benefits. Chickpea flour is an easy, no-fuss substitution for the all-purpose variety.

MAKES 25 energy cookies, 1 oz (30 g) each
OVEN TEMPERATURE: 350°F (180°C)
COOKING TIME: 15 minutes

½ cup (150 g) date puree
½ cup (150 g) unsweetened applesauce
½ cup (150 g) natural peanut butter
¼ cup (60 ml) cold water
1 egg

¼ teaspoon (1 ml) baking soda
1 tablespoon (15 ml) baking powder
Pinch of salt

1 cup (100 g) chickpea flour
1 cup (150 g) peanuts, chopped

The OMG It's So Good

(peanut, almond, and chocolate cookies)

This recipe contains no flour, gluten, or dairy, but it's still full of joyski! Caution: it's so good, it might even be joyfully addictive.

MAKES 28 energy cookies, 1 oz (30 g) each
OVEN TEMPERATURE: 350°F (180°C)
COOKING TIME: 15 minutes

½ cup (150 g) date puree
½ cup (150 g) unsweetened applesauce
½ cup (150 g) natural peanut butter
1 egg

1½ teaspoons (7 ml) baking powder
Pinch of salt

½ cup (50 g) cocoa powder
¾ cup (75 g) almond flour
¼ cup (40 g) chia seeds
½ cup (75 g) peanuts, chopped
½ cup (100 g) 75% cocoa content dark chocolate chips

All recipes pictured on page 63

The You Pecan't Stop

(graham cracker crumb, oat, and pecan cookies)

Yes, we said it. If you like pecan, I'm sure you "pecan't" resist this cookie! It's a source of fiber, energy, and intensely wonderful flavor.

MAKES 22 energy cookies, 1 oz (30 g) each
OVEN TEMPERATURE: 350°F (180°C)
COOKING TIME: 15 minutes

½ cup (150 g) date puree
½ cup (150 g) unsweetened applesauce
1 egg

¼ teaspoon (1 ml) baking soda
1 tablespoon (15 ml) baking powder
Pinch of salt

1 cup (150 g) oat flour
1 cup (90 g) graham cracker crumbs
½ cup (60 g) pecans, coarsely chopped

And then what? ● · · · · · · · · · · · · ▶

1 Preheat the oven to 350°F (180°C).
2 In a bowl, combine the ingredients from the **orange** section.
3 Add the ingredients from the blue section. Wait for a light frothing to occur (just for fun), then mix well.
4 Gradually mix in the ingredients from the **pink** section until combined.
5 Line a baking sheet with parchment paper or a silicone mat—otherwise, everything will stick.
6 Drop spoonfuls of dough to create beautifully round energy cookies, and decorate as desired.
7 Bake for about 15 minutes. Transfer the baked cookies to a cooling rack, and bask in their mouthwatering aroma.

They say life is a marathon!

Fuel your day with my energy treats!

The Just How I Like It

(multiseed and peanut bars)

Its name says it all: this bar is just how I like it, which is to say, 100% healthy. Say goodbye to store-bought chewy bars, and enjoy this extremely easy-to-make recipe. Make sure to give some to your best friends!

MAKES 10 energy bars, 1½ oz (45 g) each
OVEN TEMPERATURE: 350°F (180°C)　**COOKING TIME:** 15 minutes

½ cup (150 g) date puree
½ cup (150 g) natural peanut butter
1 egg

¾ cup (75 g) quick-cooking rolled oats
¼ cup (30 g) sesame seeds
¼ cup (40 g) chia seeds
1 cup (120 g) shelled sunflower seeds
½ cup (75 g) peanuts, chopped
¼ cup (50 g) carob chips or chocolate chips
¼ cup (55 g) Reese's pieces (optional)

And then what?

1 Preheat the oven to 350°F (180°C).
2 In a bowl, combine the ingredients from the **orange** section.
3 Gradually mix in the ingredients from the **blue** section until combined.
4 Line a baking sheet with parchment paper or with a silicone mat—otherwise, everything will stick.
5 Using a spoon, spread the mixture onto the baking sheet. Don't be afraid to firmly press it down onto the baking sheet so the bars hold together.
6 Bake for about 15 minutes. OMG! It smells so good!
7 Let cool before slicing into bars or whichever fun shape you want.

The Crunchy Energy

(cornflake and peanut butter bars)

Who doesn't like a good crunch? As long as we're making bars, we might as well set the bar highski! Lots of readers write to me saying how much they love bringing these on hikes. They're a source of fiber and leave you wanting more!

MAKES 8 energy bars, 1¾ oz (50 g) each
OVEN TEMPERATURE: 350°F (180°C)   **COOKING TIME:** 15 minutes

½ cup (150 g) date puree
¼ cup (75 g) natural peanut butter
1 egg

2 cups (30 g) cornflakes
2 tablespoons (30 ml) black chia seeds
½ cup (60 g) pecans, coarsely chopped
½ cup (65 g) raisins

And then what?

1   Preheat the oven to 350°F (180°C).
2   In a bowl, combine the ingredients from the **orange** section.
3   Add the ingredients from the **blue** section and stir to combine.
4   Line a baking sheet with parchment paper or a silicone mat—otherwise, everything will stick.
5   Using a spoon, spread the mixture onto the baking sheet. Don't be afraid to firmly press it down onto the baking sheet so the bars hold together.
6   Bake for about 15 minutes.
7   Let cool before slicing into bars or whichever fun shape you want. Going on a hike? Bring several bars along . . . your friends will love you!

The Rice and Shine

(puffed rice and almond butter bars)

Crazy! This recipe is pure culinary madness. As reinvigorating as
it is quick and easy to make, it provides you with a healthy option
to use that big box of puffed rice cereal. And besides, puffed rice
is the perfect pocket-sized source of fiber and energy.

MAKES 8 energy bars, 1¾ oz (50 g) each
OVEN TEMPERATURE: 350°F (180°C)   **COOKING TIME:** 15 minutes

½ cup (150 g) date puree
¼ cup (75 g) natural almond butter
1 tablespoon (15 ml) pure almond
    extract
1 egg

2 cups (40 g) puffed rice, or 3⅓ cups
    (100 g) puffed rice-style cereal
2 tablespoons (30 ml) chia seeds
¼ cup (25 g) almond flour
¾ cup (75 g) slivered almonds

And then what?

1   Preheat the oven to 350°F (180°C).
2   In a bowl, combine the ingredients from the
    orange section.
3   Add the ingredients from the **blue** section
    and mix until combined.
4   Line a baking sheet with parchment paper or
    a silicone mat—otherwise, everything will stick.
5   Using a spoon, spread the mixture onto the
    baking sheet. Don't be afraid to firmly press it
    down onto the baking sheet so the bars hold
    together.
6   Bake for about 15 minutes. A delightful aroma
    will soon sweep through the kitchen.
7   Let cool before slicing into bars or whichever
    fun shape you want.

The Blow Your Mind

(prune and walnut cake)

This cake knocks me to the floor. Filled with pieces of dried plums and walnuts, every slice is a filling and delicious snack. Make it now, and it will blow your mind!

MAKES one 12 x 5-inch (30 x 13 cm) cake
OVEN TEMPERATURE: 350°F (180°C)   **COOKING TIME:** 50 minutes

½ cup (150 g) date puree
½ cup (150 g) unsweetened applesauce
1 cup (250 ml) cold water
1 egg

1 tablespoon (15 ml) pure vanilla extract
½ teaspoon (2 ml) baking soda
1½ teaspoons (7 ml) baking powder
Pinch of salt

1½ cups (225 g) whole wheat flour
½ cup (50 g) quick-cooking rolled oats
¼ cup (40 g) chia seeds
1 cup (200 g) small dried pitted prunes
½ cup (60 g) walnuts, chopped

½ cup (60 g) walnuts, halved

And then what?

1   Preheat the oven to 350°F (180°C).
2   In a bowl, combine the ingredients from the **orange** section.
3   Add the ingredients from the **blue** section. Wait for a light frothing to occur (just for fun), then mix well.
4   Mix in the ingredients from the **pink** section until combined.
5   Lightly grease a 12 x 5-inch (30 x 13 cm) loaf pan—otherwise, everything will stick.
6   Transfer the delicious dough into the pan.
7   Have fun decorating the cake with walnuts from the **green** section.
8   Bake for about 50 minutes. Let cool before removing from the pan. Enjoy the sweet aroma of your freshly baked creation.

The Slice of Sunshine

(almond, apricot, and sunflower seed cake)

This gluten-free cake is a real sun-filled celebration that will make you smile. What are you eating? A slice of sunshine. What funski!

MAKES one 12 x 5-inch (30 x 13 cm) cake
OVEN TEMPERATURE: 350°F (180°C)   **COOKING TIME:** 40 minutes

½ cup (150 g) date puree
½ cup (150 g) frozen orange juice
    concentrate
1 egg

1 tablespoon (15 ml) pure almond
    extract
½ teaspoon (2 ml) baking soda
1½ teaspoons (7 ml) baking powder
Pinch of salt

1¼ cups (165 g) quinoa flour
½ cup (50 g) almond flour
¼ cup (40 g) chia seeds
½ cup (60 g) shelled sunflower seeds
1 cup (200 g) sliced dried apricots, plus
    extra for garnish
½ cup (50 g) slivered almonds

And then what?

1   Preheat the oven to 350°F (180°C).
2   In a bowl, combine the ingredients from the **orange** section.
3   Add the ingredients from the **blue** section. Wait for a light frothing to occur (just for fun), then mix well.
4   Gradually mix in the ingredients from the **pink** section until combined.
5   Lightly grease a 12 x 5-inch (30 x 13 cm) loaf pan—otherwise, everything will stick.
6   Transfer the delicious dough into the pan.
7   Decorate the cake with a few slices of dried apricots.
8   Bake for about 40 minutes. Let cool before removing from the pan and slicing.
9   Enjoy the sweet aroma of your freshly baked creation. Aren't those cake slices just magnificent?

I Feel Like Running a Marathon!

Do you need a good dose of energy, quickly? Here are some filling and energizing recipes. They're nut-free and easy to digest, which can promote high performance when working out or just at work. I like eating them before heading to a workout, in the morning, after lunch, in the evening, or simply when I need a little pick-me-up. The Pump It Up (see page 84) gives my muscles lots of energy, and the Miss Oatykins (see page 88) is a classic oatmeal treat, which I hope will become a star of your packed lunches.

On your mark, get set, bake!

4

Recipes for Your Pre-Workout Routine

The Marathon Runner

(date cookies)

Created in memory of the events of the 2013 Boston Marathon.

With their date filling, I think these date pops are really fun. They're a perfect blend of both types of carbohydrates: slow-release (flour) and quick-release (dates). Inspired by popular store-bought chewy fig-filled treats, this recipe will make you a winner.

MAKES 20 energy cookies   **OVEN TEMPERATURE:** 350°F (180°C)   **COOKING TIME:** 15 minutes

½ cup (150 g) date puree
½ cup (150 g) nonfat plain yogurt
1 egg

1 tablespoon (15 ml) pure vanilla extract
½ teaspoon (2 ml) baking soda
1½ teaspoons (7 ml) baking powder
1 teaspoon (5 ml) ground ginger
Pinch of salt

1½ cups (225 g) oat flour

20 (or more) whole dried pitted dates

And then what?

1   Preheat the oven to 350°F (180°C).

2   In a bowl, combine the ingredients from the **orange** section.

3   Add the ingredients from the **blue** section. Wait for a light frothing to occur (just for fun), then mix well.

4   Mix in the flour from the **pink** section until combined.

5   Line a baking sheet with parchment paper or a silicone mat—otherwise, everything will stick.

6   Using two spoons, dip 1 date from the **green** section into the batter, covering it with a thin layer of the batter. Transfer the date to the baking sheet. Repeat to prepare the remaining dates.

7   Bake for about 15 minutes. Transfer the cookies to a cooling rack and let cool before devouring them. Have a good workout!

The Pump It Up

(dried fruit cookies)

This high-energy, healthy cookie provides an explosion of quick-release carbs! I came up with it when I was training for the Philadelphia Marathon, and it's now one of my favorite energy cookies. Enjoy a few for a maximum energy boost!

MAKES 12 to 15 energy cookies, about 1 oz (30 g) each
OVEN TEMPERATURE: 350°F (180°C) **COOKING TIME:** 15 minutes

½ cup (150 g) date puree
½ cup (150 g) unsweetened applesauce
1 egg

1 tablespoon (15 ml) pure vanilla extract
½ teaspoon (2 ml) baking soda
1½ teaspoons (7 ml) baking powder
Finely grated zest of 1 orange
Pinch of salt

1 cup (150 g) white pastry flour
1 cup (160 g) large dried mango pieces
½ cup (80 g) dried cherries
1 cup (160 g) large dried apple pieces

And then what?

1   Preheat the oven to 350°F (180°C).
2   In a bowl, combine the ingredients from the **orange** section.
3   Add the ingredients from the **blue** section. Wait for a light frothing to occur (just for fun), then mix well.
4   Mix in the ingredients from the **pink** section until combined.
5   Line a baking sheet with parchment paper or a silicone mat—otherwise, everything will stick.
6   Drop spoonfuls of dough to create beautifully round energy cookies.
7   Bake for about 15 minutes. *Mamma mia,* those are delightful cookies!

TIPSKI!

Mix up your choice
of dried fruits!

The Teddy Bear Paw

(Bear Paws–style molasses cookies)

This cookie is perfect for school-age children. Its name is fun, and children adore it. You'll be a roaring success with these cute little pawskis! They're also a source of fiber, quick-release carbs, and iron.

MAKES 15 energy cookies, 2 oz (60 g) each
OVEN TEMPERATURE: 350°F (180°C)   **COOKING TIME:** 15 minutes

¾ cup (225 g) date puree
½ cup (150 g) nonfat plain yogurt
¾ cup (185 ml) blackstrap or fancy
   molasses
1 egg

1 tablespoon (15 ml) pure vanilla extract
¼ teaspoon (1 ml) baking soda
2 teaspoons (10 ml) baking powder
Pinch of salt

2½ cups (375 g) whole grain spelt or
   whole wheat flour
½ cup (60 g) ground flaxseeds

And then what?

1   Preheat the oven to 350°F (180°C).
2   In a bowl, combine the ingredients from the **orange** section.
3   Add the ingredients from the **blue** section. Wait for a light frothing to occur (just for fun), then mix well.
4   Gradually mix in the ingredients from the **pink** section until combined.
5   Line a baking sheet with parchment paper or a silicone mat—otherwise, everything will stick.
6   Drop spoonfuls of dough to create the paws.
7   Bake for about 15 minutes. Let the cookies cool completely before devouring.

The Miss Oatykins

(classic oat cookies)

Put this fiber- and carb-packed cookie in your little athletes' school lunches. These cookies contain no added sugar or fat and are dairy-free, peanut-free, and nut-free. This treat will give them 100% energy!

MAKES 8 to 10 energy cookies, about 2 oz (60 g) each
OVEN TEMPERATURE: 350°F (180°C)   **COOKING TIME:** 15 minutes

½ cup (150 g) date puree
½ cup (150 g) unsweetened applesauce
1 egg

1 tablespoon (15 ml) pure vanilla extract
½ teaspoon (2 ml) baking soda
1½ teaspoons (7 ml) baking powder
1½ teaspoons (7 ml) ground cinnamon
Pinch of salt

1 cup (150 g) oat flour
¾ cup (75 g) quick-cooking rolled oats
2 tablespoons (30 ml) ground flaxseeds
   or chia seeds
½ cup (65 g) raisins or dried cranberries

And then what?

1   Preheat the oven to 350°F (180°C).
2   In a bowl, add all the ingredients from the **orange** section, then mix well.
3   Add the ingredients from the **blue** section. Wait for a light frothing to occur (just for fun), then mix well.
4   Mix in the ingredients from the **pink** section until combined.
5   Line a baking sheet with parchment paper or a silicone mat—otherwise, everything will stick.
6   Drop spoonfuls of dough to create beautifully round energy cookies and decorate as desired.
7   Bake for about 15 minutes. Set aside to cool. It's soon gonna smell good . . . which means you'll soon make people happy!

The Pretty Juicy Juice

(dried fruit bars)

Have a craving for fruit juice? You're going to love these quick and easy bars packed with dried fruits. They're an ideal snack for your kids' packed lunches, or for parents and athletes who desire an energy-boosting snack.

MAKES 12 bars, 1½ to 1¾ oz (45 to 50 g) each
OVEN TEMPERATURE: 350°F (180°C)   **COOKING TIME:** 20 minutes

½ cup (150 g) date puree

1 egg

½ teaspoon (2 ml) ground ginger

½ cup (65 g) raisins

½ cup (65 g) golden raisins

½ cup (65 g) dried cranberries or ½ cup (80 g) cherries

½ cup (50 g) large flake oats

¼ cup (35 g) regular or gluten-free all-purpose flour

¼ cup (40 g) black chia seeds

And then what?

1   Preheat the oven to 350°F (180°C).

2   In a bowl, combine all the ingredients from the **orange** section and mix until combined.

3   Line a baking sheet with parchment paper or a silicone mat—otherwise, everything will stick.

4   Using a spoon, spread the mixture onto the baking sheet. Don't be afraid to firmly press it down onto the baking sheet so the bars hold together.

5   Bake for about 20 minutes. OMG! It smells so good!

6   Let the bars cool before slicing. Enjoy this fruity delight!

The Date with Destiny

(pecan and date muffins)

Is it possible to get a super healthy, energy-packed, and really tasty muffin all at once? Yes! When you have a date with destiny, you'll swoon and only have one word to say: wowski!

MAKES 12 muffins **OVEN TEMPERATURE:** 350°F (180°C) **COOKING TIME:** 42 minutes

½ cup (150 g) date puree
½ cup (150 g) unsweetened applesauce
1 ¼ cups (310 ml) cow's, almond, or soy milk
2 eggs

1 tablespoon (15 ml) pure vanilla extract
¼ teaspoon (1 ml) baking soda
1 tablespoon (15 ml) baking powder
1 ½ teaspoons (7 ml) ground cinnamon
Pinch of salt

1 cup (150 g) pastry flour
¼ cup (40 g) chia seeds
¾ cup (100 g) dried pitted dates, chopped
½ cup (60 g) chopped pecans

6 pecans, halved

And then what?

1   Preheat the oven to 350°F (180°C).
2   In a bowl, combine the ingredients from the **orange** section.
3   Add the ingredients from the blue section. Wait for a light frothing to occur (just for fun), then mix well.
4   Mix in the ingredients from the **pink** section until combined.
5   Line a muffin pan with parchment paper or silicone liners. If you don't have liners, lightly grease the pan—otherwise, everything will stick.
6   Divide the mixture evenly among the muffin cups.
7   Decorate each muffin with a pecan half from the green section.
8   Bake for about 42 minutes. Let cool. These muffins are best enjoyed once they are cooled to room temperature. Smells good!

The Un-fig-ettable

(fig, prune, and cardamom muffins)

If you love dried figs, you'll be in heaven. With the Un-fig-ettable, there are so many big chunks of fruit, it's not a fig muffin, but rather a muffin fig! They're gluten-free and dairy-free, so you can fig-et about it. (Ha ha!)

MAKES 12 muffins   **OVEN TEMPERATURE:** 350°F (180°C)   **COOKING TIME:** 40 minutes

½ cup (150 g) date puree
½ cup (150 g) unsweetened applesauce
1¼ cups (310 ml) cow's, almond, or soy milk
2 eggs

½ teaspoon (2 ml) baking soda
1 tablespoon (15 ml) baking powder
2 teaspoons (10 ml) ground cardamom
Pinch of salt

1 cup (150 g) corn flour
¼ cup (40 g) chia seeds
1 cup (130 g) dried figs, chopped, plus extra for garnish
½ cup (100 g) dried pitted prunes, chopped, plus extra for garnish

And then what?

1   Preheat the oven to 350°F (180°C).
2   In a bowl, combine the ingredients from the **orange** section.
3   Add the ingredients from the **blue** section. Wait for a light frothing to occur (just for fun), then mix well.
4   Gradually mix in the ingredients from the **pink** section (except the extra figs or prunes) and stir until combined.
5   Line a muffin pan with parchment paper or silicone liners. If you don't have liners, lightly grease the pan—otherwise, everything will stick.
6   Divide the mixture evenly among the muffin cups.
7   Decorate the muffins with large pieces of figs or prunes.
8   Bake for about 40 minutes. Don't let yourself die of hunger . . . but wait until the muffins are cool before eating them!

The Handful of Dried Fruits

(dried fruit mix)

This one isn't a recipe. This is what I do when I run out of
energy cookies at home but am still looking for something quick to eat before working out.

The easiest thing to do is stuff my pockets with some dates and go at it—you do
have a whole bag of dates in your pantry, after all! But what if you don't like how
they taste on their own? (As I've said before, date puree has a very neutral flavor,
and recipes don't taste like dates unless they're the star of the show.) Don't
worry—you can choose any other dried fruit!

Personally, I love snacking on big chunks of dried mango. I also admit I can
gobble up full bags of raisins like a champion. Sure, they contain sugar, but you
need energy to deal with life.

Oof! My muscles are hungry!

Just finished working out? Way to go! You now have 30 minutes to feed your muscles and help them maximize their recovery time. Think this is a challenge? Not with my workout-recovery recipes! They're full of carbs and proteins—yes, just like a glass of chocolate milk. These recipes are homemade solutions packed with protein to feed your muscles as well as your goals—athletic or otherwise.

Go, go, goski!

5

Recipes for Post-Workout Recovery

The Bonhomme Carnaval

(coconut cookies)

This recipe is one of the top 10 Madame Labriski energy cookies. These workout-recovery cookies are a source of protein and of joy, and were created to salute the efforts of the athletes who take part in the Quebec Winter Carnival festivities. These energy cookies are a pure delight to munch after working out, or whenever you're feeling hungry!

MAKES 24 energy cookies, 1 oz (30 g) each
OVEN TEMPERATURE: 350°F (180°C)   **COOKING TIME:** 12 minutes

½ cup (150 g) date puree
⅓ cup (100 g) nonfat plain yogurt
1 egg

1 to 2 teaspoons (5 to 10 ml) pure almond extract, to taste
½ teaspoon (2 ml) baking soda
1 teaspoon (5 ml) baking powder
Pinch of salt

1 cup (100 g) quick-cooking rolled oats
½ cup (50 g) undiluted powdered skim milk
½ cup (50 g) almond flour
2 cups (200 g) unsweetened shredded coconut
½ cup (100 g) 75% cocoa content dark chocolate chips (optional)

And then what?

1   Preheat the oven to 350°F (180°C).
2   In a bowl, combine the ingredients from the **orange** section.
3   Add the ingredients from the **blue** section. Wait for a light frothing to occur (just for fun), then mix well.
4   Mix in the ingredients from the **pink** section until combined.
5   Line a baking sheet with parchment paper or a silicone mat—otherwise, everything will stick.
6   Drop spoonfuls of dough to create beautifully round energy cookies.
7   Bake for about 12 minutes. Yum, it smells so good!

The ChocoGo

(chocolate cookies)

This cookie is a champion! It can replace the good old post-workout glass of chocolate milk. Bursting with chocolate, it gets its name from the Chicago Marathon.

MAKES 15 energy cookies, 1 oz (30 g) each
OVEN TEMPERATURE: 350°F (180°C)   **COOKING TIME:** 15 minutes

½ cup (150 g) date puree
⅓ cup (100 g) nonfat plain yogurt
1 egg

1 tablespoon (15 ml) pure vanilla extract
½ teaspoon (2 ml) baking soda
1 teaspoon (5 ml) baking powder
Pinch of salt

1½ cups (150 g) undiluted powdered
  skim milk
¾ cup (75 g) cocoa powder
¼ cup (25 g) almond flour
¼ cup (30 g) ground flaxseeds
½ to 1 cup (100 to 200 g) 75% cocoa
  content dark chocolate chips

Dark chocolate chips or discs, for
  garnish

And then what?

1   Preheat the oven to 350°F (180°C).
2   In a bowl, combine the ingredients from the **orange** section.
3   Add the ingredients from the **blue** section. Wait for a light frothing to occur (just for fun), then mix well.
4   Mix in the ingredients from the **pink** section until combined.
5   Line a baking sheet with parchment paper or a silicone mat—otherwise, everything will stick.
6   Drop spoonfuls of dough to create beautifully round energy cookies.
7   Decorate with chocolate chips or discs.
8   Bake for about 15 minutes. I'm telling you: these cookies will make you happy after each workout. Go, go, go!

The Gorrrrilla

(soy and molasses cookies)

I love combining molasses and soy. It creates such crazily delicious treats. I recommend eating this source of fiber and protein whenever you're feeling hungry. To triple the iron content, use blackstrap molasses. Grrr!

MAKES 19 energy cookies, 1 oz (30 g) each
OVEN TEMPERATURE: 350°F (180°C)
COOKING TIME: 15 minutes

½ cup (150 g) date puree
½ cup (150 g) nonfat plain yogurt
½ cup (125 ml) blackstrap or fancy molasses
1 egg

1 teaspoon (5 ml) pure vanilla extract
½ teaspoon (2 ml) baking soda
1 teaspoon (5 ml) baking powder
1 teaspoon (5 ml) ground cinnamon
1 teaspoon (5 ml) ground ginger
Pinch of salt

1½ cups (225 g) soy flour
1 cup (100 g) undiluted powdered skim milk
½ cup (60 g) ground flaxseeds
½ cup (65 g) raisins

The vVO_2max of My Dreams

(caramel and oat cookies)

What on earth is vVO_2max, you ask? It stands for "velocity at maximal oxygen uptake," which a person reaches when they're running at 100% of their ability for five to six minutes. The higher your vVO_2max, the faster you can go. With your vVO_2max, anything is possible.

MAKES 15 energy cookies, 1 oz (30 g) each
OVEN TEMPERATURE: 350°F (180°C)
COOKING TIME: 15 minutes

½ cup (150 g) date puree
½ cup (150 g) nonfat plain yogurt
1 egg

2 teaspoons (10 ml) pure vanilla extract
½ teaspoon (2 ml) baking soda
2 teaspoons (10 ml) baking powder
½ teaspoon (2 ml) ground ginger
¼ teaspoon (1 ml) ground cinnamon
Pinch of salt

One 0.1 oz (3 g) packet of caramel frosting
    mix (optional)
½ cup (75 g) oat flour
1½ cups (150 g) undiluted powdered skim
    milk
1 cup (100 g) quick-cooking rolled oats
¼ cup (30 g) ground flaxseeds
1 cup (130 g) raisins
½ to 1 cup (100 to 200 g) butterscotch
    chips (optional)

The Lemon Pie

(lemon pie cookies)

I just love lemons! Who said you could use lemon pie mix only to make a lemon pie? Have fun with these lemon pie cookies!

MAKES 12 small energy cookies
OVEN TEMPERATURE: 350°F (180°C)
COOKING TIME: 15 minutes

¼ cup (75 g) date puree
½ cup (150 g) nonfat plain yogurt
1 egg

1 package lemon pie filling mix
½ teaspoon (2 ml) baking soda
1 teaspoon (5 ml) baking powder
Pinch of salt

¾ cup (115 g) all-purpose flour
½ cup (50 g) undiluted powdered skim milk
1 tablespoon (15 ml) black chia seeds
5 to 10 drops yellow food coloring (optional)

And then what? ● ● ● ● ● ● ● ● ● ● ● ● ▶

1 Preheat the oven to 350°F (180°C).
2 In a bowl, combine the ingredients from the **orange** section.
3 Add the ingredients from the blue section. Wait for a light frothing to occur (just for fun), then mix well.
4 Mix in the ingredients from the **pink** section until combined.
5 Line a baking sheet with parchment paper or a silicone mat—otherwise, everything will stick.
6 Drop spoonfuls of dough to create beautifully round energy cookies.
7 Bake for about 15 minutes.
8 Transfer the baked cookies to a cooling rack, and bask in their mouthwatering aroma. Yum, yum, yum! These are the best post-workout treats.

The One Tough Nut-ty Cookie

(peanut butter chip cookies)

To maximize your recovery, eat this treat within 30 minutes of finishing your workout. They're so good, you'll almost feel guilty. Yet another reason to get active. Yum-yum-yumski!

MAKES 16 energy cookies, 1 oz (30 g) each
OVEN TEMPERATURE: 350°F (180°C)   **COOKING TIME:** 15 minutes

½ cup (150 g) date puree
½ cup (150 g) unsweetened applesauce
⅓ cup (100 g) natural peanut butter
1 egg

1½ teaspoons (7 ml) pure vanilla extract
½ teaspoon (2 ml) baking soda
1½ teaspoons (7 ml) baking powder
Pinch of salt

1 cup (150 g) undiluted powdered skim milk
⅔ cup (70 g) quick-cooking rolled oats
¼ cup (30 g) ground flaxseeds
½ cup (50 g) almond flour
½ cup (110 g) Reese's peanut butter chips (optional), plus extra for garnish

And then what?

1   Preheat the oven to 350°F (180°C).
2   In a bowl, combine the ingredients from the **orange** section.
3   Add the ingredients from the **blue** section. Wait for a light frothing to occur (just for fun), then mix well.
4   Mix in the ingredients from the **pink** section except the extra peanut butter chips.
5   Line a baking sheet with parchment paper or a silicone mat—otherwise, everything will stick.
6   Drop spoonfuls of dough to create beautifully round energy cookies.
7   Decorate each cookie with peanut butter chips.
8   Bake for about 15 minutes, then transfer to a cooling rack. Enjoy those muscles!

The Fruit of Your Labor

(plant protein and banana cookies)

Just exquisite! I was looking at my tub of vanilla vegan protein powder, and I thought, "Hey, what if I made a cookie out of this?" Ta-da! Here is the result. Your efforts will be rewarded.

MAKES 15 energy cookies, 1 oz (30 g) each
OVEN TEMPERATURE: 350°F (180°C)   **COOKING TIME:** 20 minutes

½ cup (150 g) date puree
½ cup (150 g) unsweetened applesauce
1 very ripe banana, mashed
1 egg

1 tablespoon (15 ml) pure vanilla extract
1 teaspoon (5 ml) baking soda
1 tablespoon (15 ml) baking powder
Pinch of salt

½ cup (50 g) vanilla vegan protein
  powder
½ cup (65 g) quinoa flour
¼ cup (40 g) chia seeds
¼ cup (50 g) dark chocolate chips
  (optional)

And then what?

1   Preheat the oven to 350°F (180°C).
2   In a bowl, combine the ingredients from the **orange** section.
3   Add the ingredients from the **blue** section. Wait for a light frothing to occur (just for fun), then mix well.
4   Mix in the ingredients from the **pink** section until combined.
5   Line a baking sheet with parchment paper or a silicone mat—otherwise, everything will stick.
6   Drop spoonfuls of dough to create beautifully round energy cookies. Decorate as desired.
7   Bake for about 20 minutes.
8   Transfer the baked cookies to a cooling rack, and bask in their mouthwatering aroma. Treat yourself and enjoy.

The Rendez-vous at the Top

(protein isolate* and peanut butter cookies)

Woahski! Those protein powders sure have a tricky name. But once you know that this simple powder gives you 93 grams of protein per 100-gram serving, you'll realize it's a good idea to use it in baking.

MAKES 35 energy cookies, 1 oz (30 g) each
OVEN TEMPERATURE: 350°F (180°C)   **COOKING TIME:** 15 minutes

½ cup (150 g) date puree
½ cup (150 g) unsweetened applesauce
½ cup (150 g) natural peanut butter
2 tablespoons (30 ml) blackstrap or fancy molasses
1 egg

½ teaspoon (2 ml) baking soda
1 tablespoon (15 ml) baking powder
Pinch of salt

1¼ cups (125 g) whey protein
½ cup (75 g) peanuts, chopped
¼ to ½ cup (50 to 100 g) dark chocolate chips

And then what?

1   Preheat the oven to 350°F (180°C).
2   In a bowl, combine the ingredients from the **orange** section.
3   Add the ingredients from the blue section. Wait for a light frothing to occur (just for fun), then mix well.
4   Mix in the ingredients from the **pink** section until combined.
5   Line a baking sheet with parchment paper or a silicone mat—otherwise, everything will stick.
6   Drop spoonfuls of dough to create beautifully round energy cookies.
7   Bake for about 15 minutes.
8   Transfer the baked cookies to a cooling rack, and bask in their mouthwatering aroma. Enjoy and dare to reach for the highest peaks.

---

*   Lactoserum protein isolates or whey protein.

The Fruity Podium

(protein isolate*, orange, and berry cookies)

This powder with a tricky name is so efficient (93 grams of protein per 100 grams) that I had no choice but to create a fruity cookie with it. And yes, you got it right: we're using frozen orange juice concentrate in this recipe. Trust Madame Labriski!

MAKES 35 energy cookies, 1 oz (30 g) each
OVEN TEMPERATURE: 350°F (180°C)   **COOKING TIME:** 15 minutes

½ cup (150 g) date puree
½ cup (150 g) frozen orange juice
    concentrate
1 egg

½ teaspoon (2 ml) baking soda
1½ teaspoons (7 ml) baking powder
Finely grated zest of 1 orange or
    2 clementines
Pinch of salt

1 cup (100 g) whey protein
1½ cups (150 g) large flake oats
½ cup (65 g) dried cranberries
½ cup (80 g) dried cherries
¼ cup (50 g) white chocolate chips

And then what?

1   Preheat the oven to 350°F (180°C).
2   In a bowl, combine the ingredients from the **orange** section.
3   Add the ingredients from the **blue** section. Wait for a light frothing to occur (just for fun), then mix well.
4   Mix in the ingredients from the **pink** section until combined.
5   Line a baking sheet with parchment paper or a silicone mat—otherwise, everything will stick.
6   Drop spoonfuls of dough to create beautifully round energy cookies.
7   Bake for about 15 minutes.
8   Transfer the baked cookies to a cooling rack, and bask in their mouthwatering aroma. Enjoy and climb every podium!

---

*   Lactoserum protein isolates or whey protein.

The Go, Legs, Go

(tropical smoothie cookies)

Yes, you can make other things besides a smoothie with a pre-packaged frozen smoothie mix! A smoothie cookie is as crazy-sounding as it is delicious. You can find this product in the frozen juice section at your local grocery store.

MAKES 24 energy cookies, 1 oz (30 g) each
OVEN TEMPERATURE: 350°F (180°C)   **COOKING TIME:** 12 minutes

½ cup (150 g) date puree
½ cup (125 ml) frozen tropical fruit
    smoothie mix
1 egg

½ teaspoon (2 ml) baking soda
1½ teaspoons (7 ml) baking powder
Finely grated zest of 1 orange or
    ½ grapefruit
Pinch of salt

½ cup (75 g) regular or gluten-free all-
    purpose flour
2 cups (200 g) undiluted powdered
    skim milk
1 cup (100 g) almond flour
½ cup (50 g) slivered almonds

And then what?

1   Preheat the oven to 350°F (180°C).
2   In a bowl, combine the ingredients from the **orange** section.
3   Add the ingredients from the **blue** section. Wait for a light frothing to occur (just for fun), then mix well.
4   Mix in the ingredients from the **pink** section until combined.
5   Line a baking sheet with parchment paper or a silicone mat—otherwise, everything will stick.
6   Drop spoonfuls of dough to create beautifully round energy cookies.
7   Bake for about 12 minutes.
8   Transfer the baked cookies to a cooling rack, and bask in their mouthwatering aroma. Enjoy and . . . go, legs!

Work out, eat well, bake, work out again, and believe in yourself.

Live life with joy, energy, and fun!

How Chic! Tiny Treats That Make Me Feel Like I'm at a Fancy Cocktail Party.

"I can't believe they're healthy."
"I'm telling you, there's no added sugar or fat in these treats."
"That's impossible!"
"But it's true."
"Yum, they're amazing. What are they called again?"
"Energy treats by Madame Labriski!"

Do you love dinner parties? Me too! But don't you wish you could bake something that isn't too traditional or too sugary? Me too! These small and elegant treats are chic and 100% delicious. You can take them on camping trips or even serve them at a big event on a silver platter. Whether they're sweet or savory, they're worthy of being called sweets for a new generation. Somebody pinch me: eating healthily has never been so decadent! And, luckily, they are ultra-easy to make.

6

Recipes Perfect for Entertaining

The You're Cherrific

(cherry and almond cookies)

They're gluten-free and incredibly delicious. Make this recipe and everyone will think you're cherrific. Then, make them again. And again! And again, and again, party after party!

MAKES 15 energy cookies, 1 oz (30 g) each
OVEN TEMPERATURE: 350°F (180°C)   **COOKING TIME:** 15 minutes

½ cup (150 g) date puree
½ cup (150 g) unsweetened mixed berry applesauce
1 egg

1½ teaspoons to 1 tablespoon (7 to 15 ml) pure almond extract, to taste
½ teaspoon (2 ml) baking soda
1½ teaspoons (7 ml) baking powder
Pinch of salt

½ cup (65 g) quinoa flour
1½ cups (150 g) slivered almonds
¾ cup (120 g) dried cherries, plus extra for garnish
¼ cup (40 g) chia seeds
¼ cup (50 g) white chocolate chips (optional)

And then what?

1   Preheat the oven to 350°F (180°C).
2   In a bowl, combine the ingredients from the orange section.
3   Add the ingredients from the blue section. Wait for a light frothing to occur (just for fun), then mix well.
4   Mix in the ingredients from the **pink** section until combined.
5   Line a baking sheet with parchment paper or a silicone mat—otherwise, everything will stick.
6   Drop spoonfuls of dough to create beautifully round energy cookies.
7   Decorate each cookie with a dried cherry.
8   Bake for about 15 minutes. Transfer the baked cookies to a cooling rack, and bask in their mouthwatering aroma.

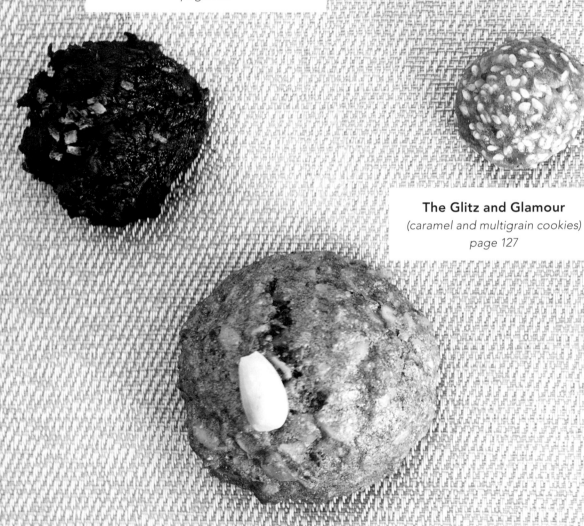

The Coconutty
(cocoa, orange, and almond cookies)
page 126

The Glitz and Glamour
(caramel and multigrain cookies)
page 127

The Amanda's Irish Surprise
(Baileys and almond cookies)
page 126

The Ex-qui-site
(chocolate cookie crumb bites)
page 129

The Date for the Ball
(date square balls)
page 128

The Smurftastic
(blueberry and almond cookies)
page 128

The Coconutty

(cocoa, orange, and almond cookies)

So classy. With their sweet orange and almond flavors, these cookies can be considered among the finest desserts. And it's true—they'll really make you go Coconutty!

MAKES 20 energy cookies, 1 oz (30 g) each
OVEN TEMPERATURE: 350°F (180°C)
COOKING TIME: 17 minutes

½ cup (150 g) date puree
½ cup (150 g) unsweetened applesauce
1 egg

¼ teaspoon (1 ml) baking soda
2 teaspoons (10 ml) baking powder
Finely grated zest of 1 large orange
Pinch of salt

½ cup (50 g) almond flour
½ cup (50 g) cocoa powder
¼ cup (30 g) ground flaxseeds
½ cup (50 g) unsweetened shredded coconut
¼ to ½ cup (50 to 100 g) 75% cocoa content dark chocolate chips

The Amanda's Irish Surprise

(Baileys and almond cookies)

If you like this famous Irish drink, you'll just love this little energy cookie. And when it's served with a small amount of Baileys on the rocks, you'll wish you had another. This recipe is a great source of fiber and . . . festive fun!

MAKES 14 energy cookies, 1 oz (30 g) each
OVEN TEMPERATURE: 350°F (180°C)
COOKING TIME: 15 minutes

½ cup (150 g) date puree
½ cup (150 g) nonfat plain yogurt
1 egg

1 to 3 teaspoons (5 to 15 ml) pure almond extract, to taste
½ cup (125 ml) Baileys
½ teaspoon (2 ml) baking soda
1 tablespoon (15 ml) baking powder
Pinch of salt

1 cup (100 g) almond flour
1 cup (150 g) whole wheat flour
1 cup (100 g) slivered almonds, chopped

All recipes pictured on page 124

The Glitz and Glamour

(caramel and multiseed cookies)

These little balls might as well put on evening gowns, as they are that chic. This gluten-free recipe is worthy of the red carpet and will make you the star of sweet yet healthy bites! Forget macarons—your guests will love these little treats instead.

MAKES 30 energy cookies, ½ oz (15 g) each
OVEN TEMPERATURE: 350°F (180°C)
COOKING TIME: 15 minutes

½ cup (150 g) date puree
1 egg
1 tablespoon (15 ml) artificial caramel extract

½ cup (75 g) gluten-free flour or another type of flour
¼ cup (40 g) chia seeds
¼ cup (30 g) ground flaxseeds
½ cup (60 g) sesame seeds

¼ cup (40 g) Skor toffee bits

And then what? ●·············▷

1   Preheat the oven to 350°F (180°C).
2   In a bowl, combine the ingredients from the **orange** section.
3   Add the ingredients from the blue section. Wait for a light frothing to occur (just for fun), then mix well.
4   Mix in the ingredients from the **pink** section until combined.
5   Line a baking sheet with parchment paper or a silicone mat—otherwise, everything will stick.
6   Drop spoonfuls of dough to create beautifully round energy cookies, and decorate as desired.
7   Bake for the time indicated. Transfer the baked cookies to a cooling rack, and bask in their mouthwatering aroma. Do I need to remind you these cookies are exquisite?

The Date for the Ball

(date square balls)

Who said date squares had to be square? This recipe is sure to be a crowd-pleaser. It's easy to make, which means you'll soon be the belle of the ballski!

MAKES 24 energy balls, 1 oz (30 g) each
OVEN TEMPERATURE: 350°F (180°C)
COOKING TIME: 12 minutes

¾ cup (225 g) date puree
1 egg

1 cup (100 g) quick-cooking rolled oats
¼ cup (40 g) chia seeds
1 cup (20 g) puffed millet

½ cup (60 g) chopped pecans
½ to 1 cup (100 to 200 g) dried pitted dates, chopped

The Smurftastic

(blueberry and almond cookies)

We sometimes take ourselves too seriously in life. The Smurftastic invites you to have a little funski! This fruity gluten- and dairy-free recipe is just Smurftastic, don't you think?

MAKES 15 energy cookies, 1 oz (30 g) each
OVEN TEMPERATURE: 350°F (180°C)
COOKING TIME: 30 minutes

½ cup (150 g) date puree
½ cup (150 g) unsweetened blueberry applesauce
1 egg

1 tablespoon (15 ml) pure almond extract
¼ teaspoon (1 ml) baking soda
½ teaspoon (2 ml) baking powder
Pinch of salt

1 cup (100 g) almond flour
½ cup (65 g) shelled green pumpkin seeds
¾ cup (75 g) slivered almonds
1 cup (150 g) dried blueberries

All recipes pictured on page 125

The Ex-qui-site

(chocolate cookie crumb bites)

OK we're cheating just a little bit by using chocolate cookie crumbs in this recipe. Am I feeling all right? It's not that at all. I just wanted to explore other recipe possibilities. So, is the result of this recipe any good? Oh, yes, it's really, really, really goooooood!

MAKES 38 energy bites, ½ oz (15 g) each
OVEN TEMPERATURE: 350°F (180°C)
COOKING TIME: 12 minutes

½ cup (150 g) date puree
½ cup (150 g) unsweetened applesauce
1 egg

1 ½ teaspoons (7 ml) baking powder
Pinch of salt

1 cup (130 g) chocolate baking cookie crumbs
¼ cup (25 g) cocoa powder
¼ cup (40 g) chia seeds
½ cup (50 g) unsweetened shredded coconut
¼ cup (50 g) 70% cocoa content dark chocolate chips

And then what? ● ● ● ● ● ● ● ● ● ● ● ● ● ▶

1. Preheat the oven to 350°F (180°C).
2. In a bowl, combine the ingredients from the **orange** section.
3. Add the ingredients from the **blue** section. Wait for a light frothing to occur (just for fun), then mix well.
4. Mix in the ingredients from the **pink** section.
5. Line a baking sheet with parchment paper or a silicone mat—otherwise, everything will stick.
6. Drop small spoonfuls of dough to create bite-sized energy balls, cookies, or bites, depending on the recipe you chose. Decorate as desired.
7. Bake for the time indicated.
8. Transfer the baked energy treats to a cooling rack, and bask in their mouthwatering aroma. Do I need to say these are ex-qui-site?

The Salty Cha-chew-chew

(cashew and sesame squares)

If you like cashews, you'll go nuts for this recipe. If you like sweet and salty food, you'll just love this one too. Everyone should try this little gem at least once. Take my word for it!

MAKES 15 energy squares, ½ oz (15 g) each
OVEN TEMPERATURE: 350°F (180°C)   **COOKING TIME:** 15 minutes

½ cup (150 g) date puree
1 egg
1 teaspoon (5 ml) artificial caramel
    extract
¼ cup (30 g) sesame seeds
1 cup (150 g) salted cashews, chopped
2 tablespoons (30 ml) Skor toffee bits
    (optional)

And then what?

1   Preheat the oven to 350°F (180°C).
2   In a bowl, add all the ingredients from the **orange** section and mix well.
3   Line a baking sheet with parchment paper or a silicone mat—otherwise, everything will stick.
4   Using a spoon, spread the dough onto the baking sheet. Don't be afraid to firmly press it down onto the pan so the squares will hold together well. Decorate with cashews if desired.
5   Bake for about 15 minutes. OMG! It smells so good!
6   Let cool before cutting into squares. Enjoy!

The Fudge My Diet!

(coffee fudge bites)

Yum, yum, yum, yum, yum, yum, yum, yum, yum, yum, yum, yum, yum, yum, yum, yum, yum, yum, yum, yum, yum, yum, yum, yum, and yumski! Need I say more? These cookies are a source of ever-lasting happiness.

MAKES 48 energy bites, ½ oz (15 g) each

OVEN TEMPERATURE: 350°F (180°C) **COOKING TIME:** 13 minutes

¾ cup (225 g) nonfat plain yogurt

½ cup (150 g) natural peanut butter

½ cup (125 ml) blackstrap or fancy molasses

1 egg

1 cup (150 g) regular or gluten-free all-purpose flour

½ cup (50 g) cocoa powder

2 tablespoons (30 ml) instant coffee

½ to 1 cup (75 to 150 g) peanuts, chopped (optional)

And then what?

1 Preheat the oven to 350°F (180°C).

2 In a bowl, add all the ingredients from the **orange** section and mix well.

3 Line a baking sheet with parchment paper or a silicone mat—otherwise, everything will stick.

4 Drop small spoonfuls of dough to create bite-sized energy balls. Decorate as desired.

5 Bake for about 13 minutes. Transfer the baked cookies to a cooling rack, and bask in their mouthwatering aroma before enjoying this guilt-free pleasure.

The Fleur de Cloud

(cocoa and fleur de sel cookies)

The Ginger Widow

(cocoa and ginger cookies)

The El Fuego

(cocoa and cayenne cookies)

Three Recipes: One Way!

One basic recipe, three incredibly flavorful, sweet treats! Whether you're in the mood for chocolatey, salty, or spicy flavors, these easy recipes look and taste like they were made by a pro.

MAKES 20 energy cookies, 1 oz (30 g) each
OVEN TEMPERATURE: 350°F (180°C)   **COOKING TIME:** 15 minutes

½ cup (150 g) date puree
½ cup (150 g) unsweetened applesauce
1 egg

¼ teaspoon (1 ml) baking soda
1½ teaspoons (7 ml) baking powder
1½ teaspoons to 1 tablespoon (7 to 15 ml) fleur de sel, ground ginger, or ground cayenne pepper (depending on the flavor of your choice, to taste)
Pinch of salt

½ cup (75 g) whole wheat flour or another type of flour
½ cup (50 g) cocoa powder
¼ cup (50 g) chocolate chips

For The Ginger Widow: ⅓ cup (35 g) chopped crystallized ginger (optional)

And then what?

1   Preheat the oven to 350°F (180°C).
2   In a bowl, combine the ingredients from the **orange** section.
3   Add the ingredients from the **blue** section corresponding to the flavor of your choice. Wait for a light frothing to occur, then mix well.
4   Mix in the ingredients from the **pink** section.
5   Line a baking sheet with parchment paper or a silicone mat—otherwise, everything will stick.
6   Drop spoonfuls of dough to create beautifully round energy cookies.
7   Decorate as desired (I like a little crystallized ginger for The Ginger Widow) from the **green** section.
8   Bake for about 15 minutes. Transfer the baked cookies to a cooling rack, and bask in their mouthwatering aroma before devouring them all.

The Effervescent

(mint chocolate cookies)

This cookie is as flavorful as the finest mint chocolates. That's rightski! It's a source of fiber and will get you lots of compliments.

MAKES 25 energy cookies, 1 oz (30 g) each
OVEN TEMPERATURE: 350°F (180°C) **COOKING TIME:** 15 minutes

½ cup (150 g) date puree
½ cup (150 g) unsweetened applesauce
1 egg

1 tablespoon (15 ml) peppermint
    extract
½ teaspoon (2 ml) baking soda
1½ teaspoons (7 ml) baking powder
Pinch of salt

1 cup (150 g) pastry flour
¾ cup (75 g) cocoa powder
½ cup (60 g) ground flaxseeds
½ cup (100 g) 75% cocoa content dark
    chocolate chips

Dark chocolate chunks (optional)

And then what?

1   Preheat the oven to 350°F (180°C).
2   In a bowl, combine the ingredients from the **orange** section.
3   Add the ingredients from the **blue** section. Wait for a light frothing to occur (just for fun), then mix well.
4   Mix in the ingredients from the **pink** section.
5   Line a baking sheet with parchment paper or a silicone mat—otherwise, everything will stick.
6   Drop spoonfuls of dough to create beautifully round energy cookies.
7   Decorate each cookie with a dark chocolate chunk, if desired.
8   Bake for about 15 minutes. Your home will soon smell heavenly!
9   Transfer to a cooling rack, and enjoy with friends.

The Salt Me Up

(caramel and fleur de sel bites)

This is one of my star recipes. Once you make it, it will become your go-to salty snack! This little treat is also a perfect hostess gift.

MAKES 20 energy bites, 1 oz (30 g) each
OVEN TEMPERATURE: 350°F (180°C)   **COOKING TIME:** 18 minutes

½ cup (150 g) date puree
½ cup (150 g) unsweetened applesauce
1 egg

2 tablespoons (30 ml) artificial caramel
    extract
½ teaspoon (2 ml) baking soda
1½ teaspoons (7 ml) baking powder
½ teaspoon (2 ml) fleur de sel, plus
    extra for garnish (optional)

1½ cups (150 g) almond flour
½ cup (50 to 60 g) flour of your choice
⅓ cup (55 g) toffee bits, plus extra for
    garnish (optional)

And then what?

1   Preheat the oven to 350°F (180°C).
2   In a bowl, combine the ingredients from the **orange** section.
3   Add the ingredients from the **blue** section. Wait for a light frothing to occur (just for fun), then mix well.
4   Mix in the ingredients from the **pink** section.
5   Line a baking sheet with parchment paper or a silicone mat—otherwise, everything will stick.
6   Drop small spoonfuls of dough to create bite-sized energy balls.
7   Sprinkle the cookies with a little extra fleur de sel or toffee bits, if desired.
8   Bake for about 18 minutes. Bask in the delightful aroma that floats around the house, enjoy, and share with friends.

The Aristocrat

(Pineau des Charentes cookies)

I love Pineau des Charentes wine, I really do. I love its aroma, its rich color, and its refined taste. Who would have thought you could make a healthy cookie using this fortified wine? Oh, you can, you canski!

MAKES 20 energy cookies, 1 oz (30 g) each
OVEN TEMPERATURE: 350°F (180°C) **COOKING TIME:** 15 minutes

1 cup (150 g) giant golden raisins, plus extra for garnish
½ cup (125 ml) white Pineau des Charentes
½ cup (150 g) date puree
⅓ cup (100 g) nonfat plain yogurt
1 egg

⅓ cup (80 ml) white Pineau des Charentes
1 tablespoon (15 ml) pure vanilla extract
½ teaspoon (2 ml) baking soda
1 tablespoon (15 ml) baking powder
Pinch of salt

2 cups (300 g) whole wheat flour
¼ cup (30 g) ground flaxseeds
⅓ cup (40 g) chopped walnuts

And then what?

1   Soak the raisins in ½ cup (125 ml) Pineau des Charentes for 12 hours.

2   The next day, preheat the oven to 350°F (180°C).

3   In a bowl, combine the raisin mixture and the ingredients from the **orange** section.

4   Add the ingredients from the **blue** section. Wait for a light frothing to occur (just for fun), then mix well.

5   Mix in the ingredients from the **pink** section.

6   Line a baking sheet with parchment paper or a silicone mat—otherwise, everything will stick.

7   Drop spoonfuls of dough to create beautifully round energy cookies. Decorate as desired.

8   Bake for about 15 minutes, then transfer to a cooling rack. Enjoy all of the reactions from your guests! They won't believe their taste buds!

The Blue Mood

(toffee bit and blueberry cookies)

This recipe was created by accident . . . but what a happy accident! You'll feel great after eating this gluten-free Blue Mood. Hurray! You simply must make these cookies at least once in your lifetime!

MAKES 15 to 18 energy cookies, about 2 oz (60 g) each
OVEN TEMPERATURE: 350°F (180°C)   **COOKING TIME:** 15 minutes

½ cup (150 g) date puree
½ cup (150 g) unsweetened applesauce
½ cup (125 ml) cow's, almond, or soy milk
1 egg

1 tablespoon (15 ml) artificial caramel extract
½ teaspoon (2 ml) baking soda
1½ teaspoons (7 ml) baking powder
Pinch of salt

⅓ cup (50 g) coconut flour
1 cup (130 g) quinoa flour
2 tablespoons (30 ml) chia seeds
½ cup (75 g) dried blueberries
¼ cup (40 g) Skor toffee bits
¼ cup (40 g) butterscotch chips

And then what?

1   Preheat the oven to 350°F (180°C).
2   In a bowl, combine the ingredients from the **orange** section.
3   Add the ingredients from the **blue** section. Wait for a light frothing to occur (just for fun), then mix well.
4   Mix in the ingredients from the **pink** section.
5   Line a baking sheet with parchment paper or a silicone mat—otherwise, everything will stick.
6   Drop spoonfuls of dough to create beautifully round energy cookies. Decorate as desired.
7   Bake for about 15 minutes, then transfer to a cooling rack. Enjoy!

The Graham-Yum

(ginger, chocolate, and graham cracker crumb bars)

When graham crackers meet ginger, the result is pure joy! Your guests will be impressed, and you'll pass for a great chef. These bars are a very intense source of happiness. Also, you can make them in next to no time.

MAKES 10 energy bars, 1½ oz (45 g) each
OVEN TEMPERATURE: 350°F (180°C)   **COOKING TIME:** 15 minutes

½ cup (150 g) date puree

1 egg

2 teaspoons (10 ml) ground ginger

1 cup (90 g) graham cracker crumbs

½ cup (50 g) quick-cooking rolled oats

½ cup (60 g) shelled sunflower seeds or nuts of your choice

¼ cup (50 g) 70% cocoa content dark chocolate chips or chunks, plus extra for garnish (optional)

And then what?

1   Preheat the oven to 350°F (180°C).

2   In a bowl, combine all the ingredients from the **orange** section.

3   Line a baking sheet with parchment paper or a silicone mat—otherwise, everything will stick.

4   Using a spoon, spread the mixture onto the baking sheet. Don't be afraid to firmly press it down onto the baking sheet so the bars hold together.

5   Decorate with additional dark chocolate chips for an elegant touch.

6   Bake for about 15 minutes. OMG! It smells so good!

7   Let cool before cutting into squares.

The Apple of My Eye

(caramel apple cake)

This cake is filled with big pieces of apple, and it's simply sensational! To save a little time, don't bother to peel the apples before slicing. Go ahead and try it out!

MAKES one 7-inch (18 cm) round cake

OVEN TEMPERATURE: 350°F (180°C)   **COOKING TIME:** 1 hour and 5 minutes

3½ cups (420 g) chopped cored apples (4 or 5 apples)
1 teaspoon (5 ml) ground cinnamon
1 tablespoon (15 ml) artificial caramel extract

¾ cup (225 g) date puree
¾ cup (225 g) unsweetened applesauce
2 eggs

1 tablespoon (15 ml) artificial caramel extract
½ teaspoon (2 ml) baking soda
1 tablespoon (15 ml) baking powder
1 tablespoon (15 ml) ground cinnamon
Pinch of salt

2 cups (300 g) pastry flour or another type of flour of your choice
¼ cup (30 g) ground flaxseeds
½ cup (60 g) chopped walnuts
¼ cup (40 g) Skor toffee bits

Apple slices, for garnish

And then what?

1 Preheat the oven to broil.
2 In a bowl, combine ingredients from the orange section.
3 Spread the mixture over a baking sheet lined with parchment paper or a silicone mat, and bake for 5 minutes. Your house will smell heavenly! Set aside to cool.
4 Preheat the oven to 350°F (180°C).
5 In a bowl, combine the ingredients from the blue section.
6 Add the ingredients from the **pink** section. Wait for a light frothing to occur (just for fun), then mix well until combined.
7 Mix in the ingredients from the green section and the baked apples.
8 Lightly grease a 7-inch (18 cm) round cake pan —otherwise, everything will stick.
9 Transfer the delicious dough to the pan.
10 Decorate with apple slices.
11 Bake for about 1 hour. Let cool before removing from the pan. This cake is a guaranteed hit!

Care for Dessert? Yes, Please— Every Night of the Week!

Do you like finishing off your meal on a sweet note? Excellent. With these energy treats, eating healthily is a sweet choice.

Don't tell my husband or my sweets-loving children that these are actually healthy. They think they're having desserts every night. Ha ha!

Go ahead and bake these—you'll be spreading joy all around!

7

Recipes for Easy Desserts

The Did Somebody Say Brownies?

(cocoa, nut, and whole grain cookies)

Wow! Just wow! Think you're in heaven? This superfood cookie is proof that eating healthily can be delicious. It's a source of fiber, antioxidants, and (you guessed it) absolute happiness.

MAKES 10 energy cookies, 1 oz (30 g) each
OVEN TEMPERATURE: 350°F (180°C)   **COOKING TIME:** 15 minutes

¾ cup (225 g) date puree
½ cup (150 g) unsweetened applesauce
¼ cup (60 ml) cow's, almond, or soy milk
1 egg

1 tablespoon (15 ml) pure vanilla extract
½ teaspoon (2 ml) baking soda
1 tablespoon (15 ml) baking powder
Pinch of salt

½ cup (75 g) whole grain spelt flour
½ cup (50 g) cocoa powder
¼ cup (30 g) ground flaxseeds
½ cup (100 g) dark chocolate chips
½ cup (60 g) chopped walnuts
¼ cup (35 g) raw cocoa nibs (optional)

Whole walnuts, for garnish

And then what?

1   Preheat the oven to 350°F (180°C).
2   In a bowl, combine the ingredients from the orange section.
3   Add the ingredients from the blue section. Wait for a light frothing to occur (just for fun), then mix well.
4   Mix in the ingredients from the **pink** section until combined.
5   Line a baking sheet with parchment paper or a silicone mat—otherwise, everything will stick.
6   Drop spoonfuls of dough to create beautifully round energy cookies.
7   Decorate each cookie with a whole walnut.
8   Bake for about 15 minutes. Transfer the baked cookies to a cooling rack, and bask in their mouthwatering aroma. Enjoy every day! This is the life!

The Chinese Almond Cookie
(almond and corn flour cookies)
page 152

The Self-Tanner
(carrot cake cookies)
page 153

The Coffee Break Anyone?
(coffee, cinnamon, and ginger cookies)
page 152

The Florida in a Tux
*(orange, poppy seed,
and dark chocolate cookies)*
page 154

The Bananaaaaaahhh
*(banana, sunflower seed,
and dark chocolate cookies)*
page 154

The Canary Island
(lemon, lime, and coconut cookies)
page 155

The Chinese Almond Cookie

(almond and corn flour cookies)

This is a healthy, gluten-free version of the famous Chinese almond cookie. It took me years and a bit of luck to find just the right combination of ingredients I wanted. And I'm thrilled-ski that I did!

MAKES 20 energy cookies, 1 oz (30 g) each
OVEN TEMPERATURE: 350°F (180°C)
COOKING TIME: 18 minutes

½ cup (150 g) date puree
½ cup (150 g) unsweetened applesauce
1 egg

1 tablespoon (15 ml) pure almond extract
½ teaspoon (2 ml) baking soda
1 tablespoon (15 ml) baking powder
Pinch of salt

½ cup (75 g) corn flour
¾ cup (75 g) almond flour

All recipes pictured on page 150

The Coffee Break Anyone?

(coffee, cinnamon, and ginger cookies)

This delicious cookie will stop time . . . or at least just enough time for a coffee break. Personally, I prefer cookie breaks or get-up-and-move breaks! What about you? Ha ha! This cookie is scrumptious and a real treatski!

MAKES 15 to 17 energy cookies, about 1 oz (30 g) each
OVEN TEMPERATURE: 350°F (180°C)
COOKING TIME: 15 minutes

½ cup (150 g) date puree
½ cup (150 g) unsweetened applesauce
1 to 2 tablespoons (15 to 30 ml) blackstrap
    or fancy molasses
1 egg

½ teaspoon (2 ml) baking soda
1 tablespoon (15 ml) baking powder
2 tablespoons (30 ml) instant coffee
1 teaspoon (5 ml) ground cinnamon
1 teaspoon (5 ml) ground ginger
1 tablespoon (15 ml) cocoa powder
Pinch of salt

1 cup (150 g) whole wheat flour
¼ cup (25 g) wheat bran
½ cup (50 g) quick-cooking rolled oats
½ cup (60 g) chopped walnuts
½ cup (65 g) Thompson raisins

The Self-Tanner

(carrot cake cookies)

My grandmother's carrot cake was delicious. This cookie is a healthier version of the classic. It's also a wonderful source of fiber and beta-carotene. The result is so orange, it looks like a bad self-tan!

MAKES 24 energy cookies, 1 oz (30 g) each
OVEN TEMPERATURE: 350°F (180°C)
COOKING TIME: 15 minutes

½ cup (150 g) date puree
½ cup (150 g) unsweetened applesauce
1 egg

1 tablespoon (15 ml) pure vanilla extract
½ teaspoon (2 ml) baking soda
1 tablespoon (15 ml) baking powder
1 tablespoon (15 ml) ground cinnamon
¼ teaspoon (1 ml) ground nutmeg
Finely grated zest of 2 oranges
Pinch of salt

½ cup (60 g) finely grated carrot (about
   1 large carrot)
2 cups (300 g) whole wheat flour
¼ cup (25 g) toasted wheat germ
1 cup (120 g) chopped walnuts
½ cup (65 g) dried currants

And then what? ●· · · · · · · · · · ➤

1. Preheat the oven to 350°F (180°C).
2. In a bowl, combine the ingredients from the **orange** section.
3. Add the ingredients from the **blue** section. Wait for a light frothing to occur (just for fun), then mix well.
4. Mix in the ingredients from the **pink** section until combined.
5. Line a baking sheet with parchment paper or a silicone mat—otherwise, everything will stick.
6. Drop spoonfuls of dough to create beautifully round energy cookies. Decorate as desired.
7. Bake for the time indicated. Transfer the baked cookies to a cooling rack, and bask in their mouthwatering aroma. Enjoy them on Mondays, Tuesdays, Wednesdays, Thursdays. . . .

The Bananaaaaaahhh

(banana, sunflower seed, and dark chocolate cookies)

I love these cookies. You pop one in your mouth and think, "Ahhh, it tastes like bananahhh!" The banana flavor can be so comforting. These cookies are a source of fiber and contagious "ahhhs"! To tell you the truth, this is one of my most beloved recipes.

MAKES 28 energy cookies, 1 oz (30 g) each
OVEN TEMPERATURE: 350°F (180°C)
COOKING TIME: 15 minutes

¾ cup (225 g) date puree
½ cup (150 g) nonfat plain yogurt
1 very ripe banana, mashed
1 egg

1 tablespoon (15 ml) pure vanilla extract
½ teaspoon (2 ml) baking soda
1 tablespoon (15 ml) baking powder
Pinch of salt

1½ cups (225 g) whole grain spelt flour, whole wheat flour, or another flour of your choice
¼ cup (30 g) ground flaxseeds
½ cup (60 g) unsalted shelled sunflower seeds
½ cup (100 g) dark chocolate chips

The Florida in a Tux

(orange, poppy seed, and dark chocolate cookies)

This is a fall cookie you can eat all year long. These cookies are a source of fiber and omega-3 fatty acids, and they're also light as air. Take a bite of these chocolatey, sunny treats. Now, do I really need to say they're full of sunshine?

MAKES 15 energy cookies, 1 oz (30 g) each
OVEN TEMPERATURE: 350°F (180°C)
COOKING TIME: 15 minutes

½ cup (150 g) date puree
½ cup (150 g) nonfat plain yogurt
1 egg

1 tablespoon (15 ml) pure vanilla extract
½ teaspoon (2 ml) baking soda
1 tablespoon (15 ml) baking powder
2 tablespoons (30 ml) poppy seeds
Finely grated zest of 3 oranges
Pinch of salt

1½ cups (225 g) spelt flour or another type of flour
2 tablespoons (30 ml) ground flaxseeds
¾ cup (150 g) dark chocolate chips

The Canary Island

(lemon, lime, and coconut cookies)

Get your fresh lemonade! The taste of this cookie is so fresh, it's like drinking lemonade from a lemonade stand.

MAKES 16 energy cookies, 1 oz (30 g) each
OVEN TEMPERATURE: 350°F (180°C)
COOKING TIME: 15 minutes

½ cup (150 g) date puree
½ cup (150 g) plain nonfat yogurt
1 egg

1 tablespoon (15 ml) pure vanilla extract
½ teaspoon (2 ml) baking soda
1 ½ teaspoons (7 ml) baking powder
Finely grated zest of 1 lemon
Finely grated zest of 2 limes
Pinch of salt

½ cup (75 g) spelt flour or another type of flour
1 cup (100 g) quick-cooking rolled oats
2 tablespoons (30 ml) ground or whole flaxseeds
½ cup (75 g) pitted dates, chopped
½ cup (60 g) chopped walnuts
¼ cup (25 g) unsweetened shredded coconut

And then what? ●●●●●●●●●●●●▶

1 Preheat the oven to 350°F (180°C).
2 In a bowl, combine the ingredients from the **orange** section.
3 Add the ingredients from the blue section. Wait for a light frothing to occur (just for fun), then mix well.
4 Mix in the ingredients from the **pink** section until combined.
5 Line a baking sheet with parchment paper or a silicone mat—otherwise, everything will stick.
6 Drop spoonfuls of dough to create beautifully round energy cookies.
7 Follow your inspiration to decorate the cookies.
8 Bake for about 15 minutes. Transfer the baked cookies to a cooling rack, and bask in their mouthwatering aroma before treating yourself.

The Smells Like Brioche

(cinnamon raisin cookies)

Yippee! These cookies will make your house smell like you just baked bread! This comforting source of fiber makes you want to treat yourself every day.

MAKES 23 energy cookies, 1 oz (30 g) each
OVEN TEMPERATURE: 350°F (180°C)   **COOKING TIME:** 15 minutes

⅔ cup (200 g) date puree
½ cup (150 g) unsweetened applesauce
3 tablespoons (45 ml) water
1 egg

½ teaspoon (2 ml) baking soda
1½ tablespoons (22 ml) baking powder
1 tablespoon (15 ml) ground cinnamon
Pinch of salt

1 cup (150 g) gluten-free flour or
   another type of flour
2 tablespoons (30 ml) chia seeds
½ cup (65 g) raisins, plus extra for
   garnish (optional)
½ cup (60 g) pecans, coarsely chopped

And then what?

1   Preheat the oven to 350°F (180°C).
2   In a bowl, combine the ingredients from the orange section.
3   Add the ingredients from the blue section. Wait for a light frothing to occur (just for fun), then mix well.
4   Mix in the ingredients from the **pink** section until combined.
5   Line a baking sheet with parchment paper or a silicone mat—otherwise, everything will stick.
6   Drop spoonfuls of dough to create beautifully round energy cookies.
7   Decorate each cookie with a raisin if desired.
8   Bake for about 15 minutes. Transfer the baked cookies to a cooling rack, and bask in their mouthwatering aroma before indulging.

The Almost–Banana Bread

(banana nut cookies)

The name says it all: this recipe is almost like banana bread—a truly healthy version of it. These Almost–Banana Bread energy cookies are a source of fiber and guilt-free indulgence. Yumski!

MAKES 28 energy cookies, 1 oz (30 g) each
OVEN TEMPERATURE: 350°F (180°C)   **COOKING TIME:** 15 minutes

¾ cup (225 g) date puree
½ cup (150 g) unsweetened applesauce
1 very ripe banana, mashed
1 egg

1 tablespoon (15 ml) pure vanilla extract
½ teaspoon (2 ml) baking soda
1½ teaspoons (7 ml) baking powder
Pinch of ground nutmeg

1½ cups (225 g) flour of your choice
   (delicious with oat flour!)
¼ cup (40 g) chia seeds
½ cup (60 g) chopped walnuts
1 large handful of raisins (optional)

And then what?

1   Preheat the oven to 350°F (180°C).
2   In a bowl, combine the ingredients from the **orange** section.
3   Add the ingredients from the blue section. Wait for a light frothing to occur (just for fun), then mix well.
4   Mix in the ingredients from the **pink** section until combined.
5   Line a baking sheet with parchment paper or a silicone mat—otherwise, everything will stick.
6   Drop spoonfuls of dough to create beautifully round energy cookies.
7   Decorate each cookie as desired.
8   Bake for about 15 minutes, then transfer to a cooling rack. Lucky you! It's going to smell like banana bread in your kitchen.

The Queen Elizabeth II

(coconut walnut cookies)

This cookie tastes like a Queen Elizabeth cake, but better: it has no added sugar or fat. It's a perfectly royal snack and a source of delightful comfort food. Curtsey for the cookie!

MAKES 22 energy cookies, 1 oz (30 g) each
OVEN TEMPERATURE: 350°F (180°C)
COOKING TIME: 15 minutes

½ cup (150 g) date puree
½ cup (150 g) unsweetened applesauce
2 eggs

2 teaspoons (10 ml) pure vanilla extract
½ teaspoon (2 ml) baking soda
1 tablespoon (15 ml) baking powder
1 tablespoon (15 ml) mixed ground
  cinnamon, nutmeg, and cloves

1 cup (150 g) flour of your choice
¼ cup (30 g) ground flaxseeds
½ cup (75 g) pitted dried dates, chopped
½ cup (60 g) chopped walnuts
½ cup (50 g) unsweetened shredded
  coconut

The Completely Gin-Gin

(graham cracker crumb ginger cookies)

When I was little, I loved gingersnaps. They're both spicy and comforting. Here's a healthy version that will make you feel completely gingersnap happy. I just love them!

MAKES 18 energy cookies, 1 oz (30 g) each
OVEN TEMPERATURE: 350°F (180°C)
COOKING TIME: 15 minutes

⅓ cup (100 g) date puree
⅓ cup (100 g) nonfat plain yogurt
1 egg

1 tablespoon (15 ml) pure vanilla extract
½ teaspoon (2 ml) baking soda
1 tablespoon (15 ml) baking powder
1 tablespoon (15 ml) ground ginger

1 cup (90 g) graham cracker crumbs
½ cup (50 g) kamut flour or another type of
  flour
2 tablespoons (30 ml) ground flaxseeds
⅓ cup (35 g) crystallized ginger, chopped

The Tipsy

(Cuban spirit and raisin cookies)

I made this recipe to use up the rum we picked up at the airport coming back from Cuba. What, you don't have any? No problem, you can use whatever spirit you've got, because you'll simply be using it for flavor. Time to get tipski!

MAKES 26 energy cookies, 1 oz (30 g) each
OVEN TEMPERATURE: 350°F (180°C)
COOKING TIME: 15 minutes

½ cup (150 g) date puree
½ cup (150 g) unsweetened applesauce
1 egg

2 tablespoons (30 ml) Ron Mulata rum (cacao liqueur)
½ teaspoon (2 ml) baking soda
1 tablespoon (15 ml) baking powder
1½ teaspoons (7 ml) ground cinnamon
1½ teaspoons (7 ml) ground ginger

1 cup (150 g) oat flour
½ cup (50 g) quick-cooking rolled oats
¼ cup (40 g) chia seeds
½ cup (65 g) raisins
½ cup (60 g) chopped walnuts
¼ cup (25 g) unsweetened shredded coconut

And then what? ● ● ● ● ● ● ● ● ● ●▶

1. Preheat the oven to 350°F (180°C).
2. In a bowl, combine the ingredients from the **orange** section.
3. Add the ingredients from the blue section. Wait for a light frothing to occur (just for fun), then mix well.
4. Mix in the ingredients from the **pink** section until combined.
5. Line a baking sheet with parchment paper or a silicone mat—otherwise, everything will stick.
6. Drop spoonfuls of dough to create beautifully round energy cookies. Decorate as desired.
7. Bake for about 15 minutes. Transfer the baked cookies to a cooling rack, and bask in their mouthwatering aroma.

The Mamahhh

(One coconut, walnut, chocolate chip, buckwheat, and raisin shareable cookie)

This is the only recipe in this book that uses buckwheat flour. This cookie should be shared because it's enormous . . . which makes it even better. One slice of The Mamahhh and everything will be all right!

MAKES 1 huge, shareable cookie   **OVEN TEMPERATURE:** 350°F (180°C)   **COOKING TIME:** 25 minutes

½ cup (150 g) date puree
½ cup (150 g) unsweetened applesauce
1 egg

1 tablespoon (15 ml) pure vanilla extract
½ teaspoon (2 ml) baking soda
1½ tablespoons (22 ml) baking powder
½ teaspoon (2 ml) ground cinnamon
Pinch of salt

1 cup (150 g) buckwheat flour
¼ cup (30 g) shelled sunflower seeds
¼ cup (25 g) unsweetened shredded
   coconut
¼ cup (35 g) raisins
¼ cup (30 g) whole walnuts
¼ cup (50 g) dark chocolate chips

And then what?

1   Preheat the oven to 350°F (180°C).
2   In a bowl, combine the ingredients from the **orange** section.
3   Add the ingredients from the **blue** section. Wait for a light frothing to occur (just for fun), then mix well.
4   Mix in the ingredients from the **pink** section until combined.
5   Line a baking sheet with parchment paper or a silicone mat—otherwise, everything will stick.
6   Spread the dough into the shape of a giant cookie.
7   Decorate as you wish: be creative!
8   Bake for about 25 minutes, then transfer to a cooling rack.
9   Share the cookie, and enjoy the moment.

The You're Nut Going to Believe It

(peanut butter mug cake à la Labriski)

This energy-packed solution is ultra-easy and quick to make (seriously, you just need 1 minute!). Treat yourself!

MAKES 1 mug cake   **COOKING TIME:** 1 minute (in the microwave)

1 tablespoon (15 ml) date puree

1 tablespoon (15 ml) egg white

1½ teaspoons (7 ml) natural peanut butter

½ teaspoon (2 ml) baking powder

1 tablespoon (15 ml) flour of your choice

1 teaspoon (5 ml) cow's, almond, or soy milk

1½ teaspoons (7 ml) chopped peanuts or chocolate chips (optional)

And then what?

1   Pick a mug with a capacity of 1 to 1¼ cups (250 to 310 ml).

2   Add all the ingredients from the **orange** section to the mug and mix until combined.

3   Microwave for 1 minute.

4   Ta-da!

The Now I Can Die Happy

(peanut butter and caramel bites)

Astounding! Decadent! Invigorating! Sublime! Thrilling! It's simple: this treat was created so you can enjoy life to the fullest. Bake it and enjoy it! If you make your bites a bit larger, increase the baking time a little.

MAKES 45 energy bites, ½ oz (15 g) each
OVEN TEMPERATURE: 350°F (180°C)   **COOKING TIME:** 12 minutes

½ cup (150 g) date puree
½ cup (155 g) natural peanut butter
1 egg
1 tablespoon (15 ml) artificial caramel extract
¼ cup (40 g) chia seeds
3 cups (48 g) puffed millet
⅓ cup (50 g) peanuts, chopped
¼ cup (40 g) Skor toffee bits

And then what?

1   Preheat the oven to 350°F (180°C).
2   In a bowl, add all the ingredients from the **orange** section and mix well.
3   Line a baking sheet with parchment paper or with a silicone mat—otherwise, everything will stick.
4   Drop small spoonfuls of dough to create bite-sized energy balls.
5   Bake for about 12 minutes. If you make larger bites, bake for an additional 3 minutes.
6   Transfer the baked cookies to a cooling rack, and bask in their mouthwatering aroma before treating yourself.

The Chop-Chop Hazelnuts

(chocolate and hazelnut cake)

This source of fiber and festive cheer is perfect for a hostess gift. Wrap some up in brown paper, tie a ribbon around it, and delight your guests! What? Is this cake really healthy? You betski!

MAKES one 12 x 5-inch (30 x 13 cm) cake
OVEN TEMPERATURE: 350°F (180°C)   **COOKING TIME:** 45 minutes

¾ cup (225 g) date puree
½ cup (150 g) unsweetened applesauce
1½ cups (375 ml) cow's, almond, or soy milk
1 egg

1 tablespoon (15 ml) pure vanilla extract
2 to 3 tablespoons (30 to 45 ml) hazelnut-flavored instant coffee
½ teaspoon (2 ml) baking soda
1 tablespoon (15 ml) baking powder
Pinch of salt

1½ cups (225 g) whole grain spelt flour
½ cup (50 g) cocoa powder
¼ cup (30 g) ground flaxseeds
¼ cup (40 g) black chia seeds
¼ to ½ cup (25 to 50 g) dark chocolate chips
1½ cups (210 g) raw whole hazelnuts (filberts), plus extra for garnish

And then what?

1   Preheat the oven to 350°F (180°C).
2   In a bowl, combine the ingredients from the **orange** section.
3   Add the ingredients from the **blue** section. Wait for a light frothing to occur (just for fun), then mix well.
4   Mix in the ingredients from the **pink** section until combined.
5   Lightly grease a 12 x 5-inch (30 x 13 cm) loaf pan—otherwise, everything will stick.
6   Transfer the delicious dough into the pan.
7   Decorate the cake with a few hazelnuts.
8   Bake for about 45 minutes. Let cool before removing from the pan.
9   Enjoy the sweet aroma of your freshly baked creation. Just to confirm: you'll soon be devouring this treat.

The Maple Crunchy Munchy

(maple syrup and puffed rice squares)

When crumbled, these squares add a little crunch to yogurt, sorbets, and other sweet treats. It's just so good with maple syrup! Crunch, crunch, crunch. . . . Crunchski!

MAKES ½ baking sheet of maple-baked crumble
OVEN TEMPERATURE: 350°F (180°C)   **COOKING TIME:** 15 to 20 minutes

2 eggs
⅔ cup (160 ml) maple syrup
2 cups (40 g) puffed rice
2 cups (240 g) unsweetened shredded coconut or 2 cups of nuts of your choice (walnuts, pecans, peanuts, etc.)

And then what?

1   Preheat the oven to 350°F (180°C).
2   In a bowl, add all the ingredients from the orange section and mix well.
3   Line a baking sheet with parchment paper or a silicone mat—otherwise, everything will stick.
4   Using a spoon, spread the mixture onto the baking sheet. Don't be afraid to firmly press it down onto the baking sheet so the squares hold together.
5   Bake for 15 to 20 minutes. OMG! It smells so good!
6   Let cool before cutting into squares. I bet these will disappear in a flash!

The Salty Chocolate Surprise

(cookie-filled cake)

This culinary creation is so much fun that it will turn heads. It breaks with conventions and encourages creativity! Happiness truly is discovering a hidden treasure: the salty chocolate cookies within this blueberry white chocolate cake!

MAKES one 7-inch (18 cm) round cake

OVEN TEMPERATURE: 350°F (180°C)   **COOKING TIME:** 1 hour and 10 minutes

10 to 14 Fleur de Cloud cookies
(1 oz/30 g each) (recipe on page 135)

¾ cup (225 g) date puree
¾ cup (225 g) unsweetened applesauce
2 tablespoons (30 ml) cold water
2 eggs

1 tablespoon (15 ml) pure vanilla extract
½ teaspoon (2 ml) baking soda
1 tablespoon (15 ml) baking powder
Pinch of salt

2 cups (300 g) pastry flour or another
type of flour of your choice
1 cup (150 g) frozen blueberries, plus
extra for garnish (optional)
½ cup (100 g) white chocolate chips,
plus extra for garnish (optional)

And then what?

1   Prepare the Fleur de Cloud cookies in advance.
2   Preheat the oven to 350°F (180°C).
3   In a bowl, combine the ingredients from the **blue** section.
4   Add the ingredients from the **pink** section. Wait for a light frothing to occur (just for fun), then mix well.
5   Mix in the ingredients from the **green** section.
6   Lightly grease a 7-inch (18 cm) round cake pan —otherwise, everything will stick.
7   Set 5 to 7 Fleur de Cloud cookies on the bottom of the cake pan, then spread half of the batter over the cookies.
8   Add 5 to 7 more Fleur de Cloud cookies, then cover with the remaining batter.
9   Decorate with blueberries and white chocolate chips if desired.
10   Bake for about 1 hour and 10 minutes. Let cool before removing from the pan. Your house will smell insanely great!
11   Slice the cake and enjoy your guests' reactions.

The Guilty Pleasure

(chocolate caramel muffins)

Is this a decadent dessert or a healthy alternative to a cupcake?
Both! This creation is breathtaking. Even I can't believe it!

MAKES 9 to 12 muffins   **OVEN TEMPERATURE:** 350°F (180°C)   **COOKING TIME:** 20 to 25 minutes

¾ cup (225 g) date puree
½ cup (150 g) unsweetened applesauce
1 cup (250 ml) cow's, almond, or soy
   milk
1 egg

1 tablespoon (15 ml) artificial caramel
   extract
½ teaspoon (2 ml) baking soda
1 tablespoon (15 ml) baking powder
Pinch of salt

1½ cups (150 g) whole grain spelt flour
½ cup (50 g) cocoa powder
⅓ cup (40 g) ground flaxseeds
¼ cup (50 g) dark chocolate chips
¼ cup (40 g) Skor toffee bits

And then what?

1   Preheat the oven to 350°F (180°C).
2   In a bowl, combine the ingredients from the
    orange section.
3   Add the ingredients from the blue section.
    Wait for a light frothing to occur (just for fun),
    then mix well.
4   Mix in the ingredients from the **pink** section
    until combined.
5   Line a muffin pan with parchment paper or sil-
    icone liners—otherwise, everything will stick.
6   Divide the mixture evenly among the muffin
    cups. Decorate with whatever garnishes you
    have on hand.
7   Bake for 20 to 25 minutes. Let cool before
    removing from the pan. Enjoy the sweet
    aroma of your freshly baked creation.

TIPSKI!

Cut open the tea bags and add the contents directly into your recipe. It's crazy good!

The E.Tea

(Tea cake)

Here's a solution for using up your old bags of tea and herbal blends! It's delicious and simple, and it helps you clean out your pantry. Time for teaski?

MAKES one 12 x 5-inch (30 x 13 cm) cake
OVEN TEMPERATURE: 350°F (180°C) **COOKING TIME:** 1 hour

½ cup (150 g) date puree
½ cup (150 g) unsweetened applesauce
¾ cup (185 ml) water
1 egg

1½ tablespoons (22 ml) dried tea or dried herbal tea mix (about 3 tea bags)
½ teaspoon (2 ml) baking soda
1 tablespoon (15 ml) baking powder
Pinch of salt

1 cup (150 g) gluten-free flour or another type of flour
½ cup (50 g) quick-cooking rolled oats
¼ cup (30 g) ground flaxseeds

And then what?

1   Preheat the oven to 350°F (180°C).
2   In a bowl, combine the ingredients from the **orange** section.
3   Add the ingredients from the **blue** section. Wait for a light frothing to occur (just for fun), then mix well.
4   Mix in the ingredients from the **pink** section until combined.
5   Lightly grease a 12 x 5-inch (30 x 13 cm) loaf pan—otherwise, everything will stick.
6   Transfer the delicious dough into the pan.
7   Bake for about 1 hour, let cool, and take a moment to bask into the mouthwatering aroma before removing the cake from the pan. Decorate as desired.
8   Slice and admit to yourself that the idea of making a tea bag cake really is a clever one! Ha! Ha! Ha!

Hooray!
It's Party Time!

Here we're breaking with tradition and adding fiber, joy, love, and a little craziness into the mix! We're serving up bold and original recipes! Are these recipes hard? Not at all. They're perfect for the holidays, but with a touch of originality. Celebrating has never been so fun!

8

Recipes for the Holidays

The Cinderella's Coach

(pumpkin and dark chocolate cookies)

Give new life to your Halloween pumpkins! For even more fun, eat up these cookies before the clock strikes midnight . . . With or without your prince! They're a source of fiber, comfort, and the sweet scent of slightly spiced pumpkin.

MAKES 20 energy cookies, 1 oz (30 g) each
OVEN TEMPERATURE: 350°F (180°C)   **COOKING TIME:** 15 minutes

2 cups (240 g) diced pumpkin flesh, plus extra for garnish

½ cup (150 g) date puree
½ cup (150 g) nonfat plain yogurt
1 egg

1 tablespoon (15 ml) pure vanilla extract
½ teaspoon (2 ml) baking soda
1½ teaspoons (7 ml) baking powder
¼ teaspoon (1 ml) ground ginger
Pinch of ground nutmeg
Finely grated zest of 1 orange
Pinch of salt

1 cup (150 g) whole grain spelt or whole wheat flour
½ cup (50 g) quick-cooking rolled oats
¼ cup (30 g) ground flaxseeds
½ cup (65 g) shelled green pumpkin seeds
¼ cup (50 g) dark chocolate chips

And then what?

1   Preheat the oven to broil.
2   Spread the pumpkin from the **orange** section over a baking sheet lined with parchment paper or a silicone mat, and bake for 5 minutes. Set aside.
3   Set the oven temperature to 350°F (180°C).
4   In a bowl, combine the ingredients from the blue section.
5   Add the ingredients from the **pink** section. Wait for a light frothing to occur (just for fun), then mix well.
6   Mix in the ingredients from the green section until combined.
7   Add the baked pumpkin and mix well.
8   Line a baking sheet with parchment paper or a silicone mat—otherwise, everything will stick.
9   Drop spoonfuls of dough to create beautifully round energy cookies.
10 Decorate as desired.
11 Bake for about 15 minutes. Transfer the baked cookies to a cooling rack, and bask in their mouthwatering aroma. Run, Cinderella, run . . . before we eat you!

The Boooooo

(chocolate Halloween cookies)

Boo! Here's a delicious way to prepare for Halloween as a family. Classics are great, but classics in a colorful disguise are even better! How about making Frankenstein-green cookies or using blood-red colors? Booooooooski!

MAKES 18 colorful energy cookies, 1 oz (30 g) each
OVEN TEMPERATURE: 350°F (180°C)   **COOKING TIME:** 15 minutes

½ cup (150 g) date puree
½ cup (150 g) unsweetened applesauce
1 egg, or ¼ cup (60 ml) almond or soy milk

1 tablespoon (15 ml) pure vanilla extract
½ teaspoon (2 ml) baking soda
1½ teaspoons (7 ml) baking powder
Pinch of salt

1 cup (150 g) flour of your choice
¼ cup (30 g) ground flaxseeds
½ to ¾ cup (100 to 150 g) dark or white chocolate chips, to taste

A few drops of food coloring of your choice (optional, but fun!)

And then what?

1   Preheat the oven to 350°F (180°C).

2   In a bowl, combine the ingredients from the **orange** section.

3   Add the ingredients from the **blue** section. Wait for a light frothing to occur (just for fun), then mix well.

4   Mix in the ingredients from the **pink** section until combined.

5   Add a few drops of food coloring and have fun creating monster cookies.

6   Line a baking sheet with parchment paper or a silicone mat—otherwise, everything will stick.

7   Drop spoonfuls of dough to create beautifully round energy cookies.

8   Bake for about 15 minutes. Transfer to a cooling rack.

9   Have fun, and watch the surprised reactions of the lucky recipients!

Recipe pictured on the title page.

The Pumpk-Incredible

(pumpkin cake)

What can you make with leftover pumpkin? You can make this delicious cake, with no added sugar, dairy, or fat, that contains more than 4 cups (520 g) of pumpkin. That's what!

MAKES one 7-inch (18 cm) round cake **OVEN TEMPERATURE:** 350°F (180°C)
COOKING TIME: about 1 hour and 20 minutes

4 cups (520 g) diced pumpkin flesh
1 teaspoon (5 ml) ground cinnamon
1 teaspoon (5 ml) ground ginger

¾ cup (225 g) date puree
¾ cup (225 g) unsweetened applesauce
2 eggs

1 tablespoon (15 ml) pure vanilla extract
½ teaspoon (2 ml) baking soda
1 tablespoon (15 ml) baking powder
1 tablespoon (15 ml) ground cinnamon
1½ tablespoons (22 ml) ground ginger
Pinch of ground nutmeg

½ cup (75 g) all-purpose flour, regular or gluten-free
1½ cups (150 g) quick-cooking rolled oats
¼ cup (30 g) ground flaxseeds
½ cup (60 g) chopped walnuts, plus extra for garnish
½ cup (65 g) raisins, plus extra for garnish
½ cup (65 g) shelled green pumpkin seeds, plus extra for garnish

And then what?

1   Preheat the oven to broil.
2   In a bowl, combine the ingredients from the **orange** section.
3   Spread the mixture over a baking sheet lined with parchment paper or a silicone mat, and bake for 5 minutes. Set aside.
4   Lower the heat to 350°F (180°C).
5   In a bowl, combine the ingredients from the **blue** section.
6   Add the ingredients from the **pink** section. Wait for a light frothing to occur (just for fun), then mix well.
7   Mix in the ingredients from the **green** section and the baked pumpkin until combined.
8   Lightly grease a 7-inch (18 cm) round cake pan —otherwise, everything will stick.
9   Transfer the delicious cake mixture into the pan.
10   Decorate with walnuts, raisins, and pumpkin seeds as desired. Have fun!
11   Bake for about 1 hour and 20 minutes. Let cool before removing from the pan.

The Santa's Special Request

(chocolate and coconut bites)

This recipe is a special request from Santa Claus. Really? Yes, he asked Madame Labriski for this recipe himself! Made with coconut flour, this chewy treat is elegant, packed with fiber, and truly delicious, to keep him flying all through the nightski!

MAKES 48 energy bites, ½ oz (15 g) each

OVEN TEMPERATURE: 350°F (180°C) **COOKING TIME:** 20 minutes

½ cup (150 g) date puree
½ cup (150 g) nonfat plain yogurt
1¼ cups (310 ml) cow's, almond, or soy
milk

1 egg
1 tablespoon (15 ml) pure vanilla
extract or pure coconut extract
¼ teaspoon (1 ml) baking soda
1½ teaspoons (7 ml) baking powder
Pinch of salt

1 cup (150 g) coconut flour (filled with
fiber and is gluten-free!)
½ cup (50 g) cocoa powder
½ cup (60 g) ground flaxseeds
½ cup (100 g) dark chocolate chips
½ cup (50 g) unsweetened shredded
coconut

About 1 cup (100 g) unsweetened
shredded coconut (to roll the bites in)

And then what?

1   Preheat the oven to 350°F (180°C).

2   In a bowl, combine the ingredients from the **orange** section.

3   Add the ingredients from the **blue** section. Wait for a light frothing to occur (just for fun), then mix well.

4   Mix in the ingredients from the **pink** section.

5   Line a baking sheet with parchment paper or a silicone mat—otherwise, everything will stick.

6   Using your hands, roll portions of dough into small balls, then roll in the shredded coconut from the **green** section. It's a sticky job, but it's worth the mess!

7   Bake for about 20 minutes. Transfer the baked cookies to a cooling rack, and bask in their mouthwatering aroma.

The Ho! Ho! How I Love Fruit!

(dried fruitcake)

Bring color to your festivities, and try this energy-packed healthy recipe. It's a refreshing version of a traditional fruitcake. A classic with the Madame Labriski twist.

MAKES one 12 x 5-inch (30 x 13 cm) cake
OVEN TEMPERATURE: 350°F (180°C) **COOKING TIME:** 50 minutes

½ cup (150 g) date puree
½ cup (150 g) unsweetened applesauce
1¼ cups (310 ml) cow's, almond, or soy milk
1 egg

1 tablespoon (15 ml) pure vanilla extract
½ teaspoon (2 ml) baking soda
1 tablespoon (15 ml) baking powder
Pinch of salt

1½ cups (225 g) oat or whole wheat flour
¼ cup (40 g) black chia seeds
⅔ cup (110 g) dried cherries
⅔ cup (90 g) dried cranberries
⅔ cup (70 g) frozen cranberries, halved
⅔ cup (55 g) dried kiwi slices, plus extra for garnish
⅔ cup (80 g) chopped walnuts
¼ cup (50 g) white chocolate chips (optional)

And then what?

1   Preheat the oven to 350°F (180°C).
2   In a bowl, combine the ingredients from the **orange** section.
3   Add the ingredients from the **blue** section. Wait for a light frothing to occur (just for fun), then mix well.
4   Gradually mix in the ingredients from the **pink** section and stir until combined.
5   Lightly grease a 12 x 5-inch (30 x 13 cm) loaf pan—otherwise, everything will stick.
6   Transfer the delicious dough into the pan.
7   Decorate the cake with dried kiwi slices, placing them to create a fir tree shape.
8   Bake for about 50 minutes. Let cool before removing from the pan.
9   Enjoy the sweet aroma of your freshly baked creation. Happy holidays!

I Love Me a Mishmash
*(white and dark chocolate chip
and coconut cookies)*
page 192

The Rudolphette
(red and white chocolate chip cookies)
page 192

The Fresh-Mallow
(strawberry and marshmallow cookies)
page 193

The Captain Snack
(caramel and pretzel cookies)
page 194

The Sunday Funday
(pecan maple syrup cookies)
page 195

The Rudolphette

(red and white chocolate chip cookies)

During the holidays, not only is Rudolph's nose red, but this seasonal cookie is as well! Think about how beautiful a tray of them will look on your holiday dessert table? Also, they're healthy, so if you're lucky you'll find some in your stocking!

MAKES 15 energy cookies, 1 oz (30 g) each
OVEN TEMPERATURE: 350°F (180°C)
COOKING TIME: 15 minutes

½ cup (150 g) date puree
½ cup (150 g) plain yogurt
1 egg

1 tablespoon (15 ml) pure vanilla extract
½ teaspoon (2 ml) baking soda
1 tablespoon (15 ml) baking powder
2 tablespoons (30 ml) cocoa powder
3 to 4 tablespoons (or more) red food
    coloring

1 cup (150 g) whole wheat flour or another
    type of flour
⅓ cup (40 g) ground flaxseeds
½ cup (100 g) white chocolate chips

The I Love Me a Mishmash

(white and dark chocolate chip and coconut cookies)

This cookie is so good, you'll be hit by Cupid's arrow and fall in love at first bite! It's also a source of fiber and full of love.

MAKES 12 to 15 energy cookies, about 1 oz (30 g) each
OVEN TEMPERATURE: 350°F (180°C)
COOKING TIME: 17 minutes

½ cup (150 g) date puree
½ cup (150 g) nonfat plain yogurt
¼ cup (60 ml) cow's, almond, or soy milk
1 egg

1 tablespoon (15 ml) pure vanilla extract
½ teaspoon (2 ml) baking soda
1½ teaspoons (7 ml) baking powder
Pinch of salt

½ cup (75 g) whole grain spelt flour
½ cup (50 g) cocoa powder
⅓ cup (35 g) wheat bran
¼ cup (30 g) ground flaxseeds
¼ cup (25 g) unsweetened shredded
    coconut
¼ cup (50 g) 75% cocoa content dark
    chocolate chips
¼ cup (50 g) white chocolate chips

All recipes pictured on page 188

The Fresh-Mallow

(strawberry and marshmallow cookies)

This idea came to me when I was coming home from a camping weekend. What can you do with leftover marshmallows? Make cookies with fresh strawberries and marshmallows, that's what! What a great, festive ideaski!

MAKES 15 energy cookies, 1 oz (30 g) each
OVEN TEMPERATURE: 350°F (180°C)
COOKING TIME: 20 minutes

½ cup (150 g) date puree
½ cup (150 g) unsweetened applesauce
1 egg

½ teaspoon (2 ml) baking soda
1½ teaspoons (7 ml) baking powder
Pinch of salt

1¼ cups (180 g) all-purpose flour, regular or gluten-free
2 tablespoons (30 ml) ground flaxseeds
1 cup (150 g) fresh strawberries, diced
1 cup (60 g) large marshmallows (9 or 10 marshmallows), diced

And then what?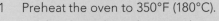

1. Preheat the oven to 350°F (180°C).
2. In a bowl, combine the ingredients from the **orange** section.
3. Add the ingredients from the blue section. Wait for a light frothing to occur (just for fun), then mix well.
4. Mix in the ingredients from the **pink** section until combined.
5. Line a baking sheet with parchment paper or a silicone mat—otherwise, everything will stick.
6. Drop spoonfuls of dough to create beautifully round energy cookies.
7. Decorate each cookie with whatever you have on hand. Be creative!
8. Bake for the time indicated. Transfer the baked cookies to a cooling rack, and bask in their mouthwatering aroma.

The Captain Snack

(caramel and pretzel cookies)

Take all of your leftover pretzels, Cajun sesame sticks, barbecue peanuts, and any other crunchy party food you have hanging around, and add them to the mix for these cookies! If you like sweet and salty flavors, you're going to love The Captain Snack!

MAKES 15 energy cookies, 1 oz (30 g) each
OVEN TEMPERATURE: 350°F (180°C)
COOKING TIME: 15 minutes

½ cup (150 g) date puree
½ cup (150 g) unsweetened applesauce
1 egg

1 tablespoon (15 ml) artificial caramel extract
½ teaspoon (2 ml) baking soda
1 tablespoon (15 ml) baking powder
Pinch of salt

1 cup (150 g) flour of your choice
¼ cup (40 g) Skor toffee bits
½ cup (50 g) pretzels or salted snack mix

TIPSKI!

Did you know pecans add a buttery taste to any recipe?

All recipes pictured on page 189

The Sunday Funday

(pecan maple syrup cookies)

Soft and comforting, this springtime creation is perfect for maple season. Like maple taffy, these cookies are even better when served cold. Brrrrrski!

MAKES 20 energy cookies, 1 oz (30 g) each
OVEN TEMPERATURE: 350°F (180°C)
COOKING TIME: 15 minutes

½ cup (150 g) date puree
½ cup (150 g) plain yogurt
½ cup (125 ml) maple syrup
1 egg

½ teaspoon (2 ml) baking soda
1 tablespoon (15 ml) baking powder
Pinch of salt

1 cup (150 g) oat flour
1 cup (150 g) whole grain spelt flour
¼ cup (30 g) ground flaxseeds
1 cup (120 g) pecans, coarsely chopped

And then what? ● · · · · · · · · · · ▶

1. Preheat the oven to 350°F (180°C).
2. In a bowl, add all the ingredients from the **orange** section, then mix well.
3. Add the ingredients from the blue section. Wait for a light frothing to occur (just for fun), then mix well.
4. Mix in the ingredients from the **pink** section and stir until combined.
5. Line a baking sheet with parchment paper or a silicone mat—otherwise, everything will stick.
6. Drop spoonfuls of dough to create beautifully round energy cookies.
7. Decorate each energy cookie as desired.
8. Bake for about 15 minutes, then transfer to a cooling rack. It's time to party!

The Maple Crunch-eanut

(maple, peanut, and oat bites)

What's this, a recipe with no date puree? Exactly. The goals are to highlight maple syrup and celebrate the return of spring. Happy! Happy! Happy!

MAKES 14 crunchy bites, 1 oz (30 g) each
OVEN TEMPERATURE: 350°F (180°C)   **COOKING TIME:** 15 minutes

1 egg
½ cup (125 ml) maple syrup
½ cup (50 g) quick-cooking rolled oats
1 cup (20 g) puffed millet
½ cup (75 g) peanuts, chopped

And then what?

1   Preheat the oven to 350°F (180°C).

2   In a bowl, add all the ingredients from the **orange** section and mix well.

3   Line a baking sheet with parchment paper or a silicone mat—otherwise, everything will stick.

4   Drop small spoonfuls of dough to create bite-sized energy balls.

5   That's it? Yep!

6   Bake for about 15 minutes.

7   Transfer the baked cookies to a cooling rack, and bask in their mouthwatering aroma. Decorate as desired. They're crunchy and taste like spring!

Thank you for baking with joy and spreading good things with my energy treats!

Index

To be continued . . .